IDENTITY CONFUSION
& the Church

A Mother's Faith Journey with Her Transgendered Child

VERA ENGLISH

Except where noted, Scripture quotations are taken from The Holy Bible, New International Version® NIV® Copyright © 1973 1978 1984 2011 by Biblica, Inc. TM. Used by permission. All rights reserved worldwide.

Scripture quotations marked (NLT) are taken from the Holy Bible, New Living Translation, copyright ©1996, 2004, 2015 by Tyndale House Foundation. Used by permission of Tyndale House Publishers, Carol Stream, Illinois 60188. All rights reserved.

Scripture marked NKJV taken from the New King James Version®. Copyright © 1982 by Thomas Nelson. Used by permission. All rights reserved.

Editor: Mary Beth Baker

Designer: KUHN Design Group

Copyright © 2021 by Vera English
All rights reserved.
ISBN: 978-1-7377427-0-8
Published by FarmHousePress

Dedicated to the beautiful lilies of the world.

CONTENTS

Introduction 7

Chapter 1—Muddled Identities 11

Chapter 2—Back to the Beginning 23

Chapter 3—A New Design 35

Chapter 4—You've Got a Friend in Me 49

Chapter 5—The Way of Abiding 67

Chapter 6—Freedom to Love Jesus 81

Chapter 7—Fighting the Good Fight 95

INTRODUCTION

INTRODUCTION

As a mom—and a Christian—I never imagined facing the heart-wrenching trial of identity confusion in one of my children. It simply was not on my radar, certainly not to the degree that it manifested itself in my daughter, Lily. I soon came to realize that alternative identity exploration is a growing societal phenomenon. But what exactly is it, and why is this happening in Christian families?

Amazingly, what started out as a quest to understand identity confusion from a biblical perspective shifted into a rescue mission of my own faith. There is no greater wake-up call for the church than to discover that our children feel safer and more at home in the world's definition of meaning and purpose.

Yet the question remains, what is prompting an entire generation to abandon their Christian upbringing for alternative realities that feel like a better fit?

In this book, I not only address this critical question, but share my personal story of how God allowed the hardship of identity confusion to bring me sobering clarity regarding deep matters of faith.

While the book's contents are reflective of my own journey, I pray that these pages serve to encourage any who find themselves navigating similar life complexities.

The reality is that identity confusion provides great opportunity to ask ourselves why we believe the things we do. Our faith becomes more precious when we plunge beneath the surface of mere theological constructs to explore the gravity of the cross on a personal level. God, knowing that we would be living in these times, has good news remarkably applicable to identity. Join me as we explore the freedom that comes from a fresh look at the Gospel in an identity confused world.

> *"I will love them freely..."*
> **HOSEA 14:4, NKJV**

CHAPTER 1

MUDDLED IDENTITIES

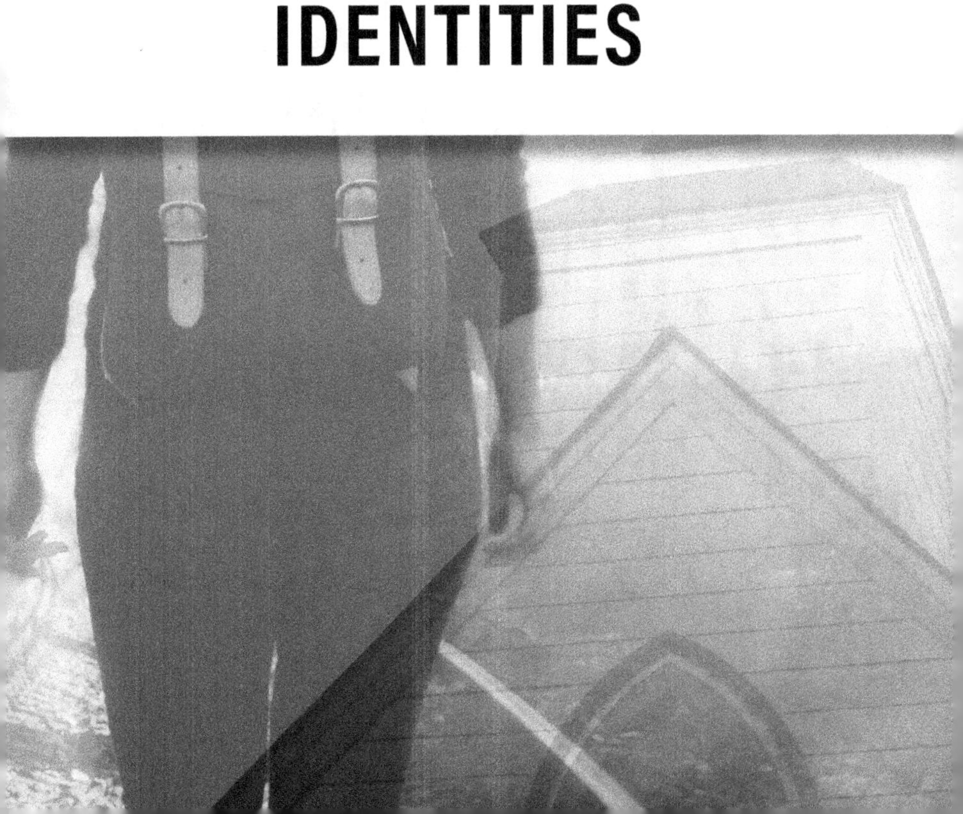

I have to be honest—when my daughter announced that she would be identifying as a male, it felt like the bottom of my world fell through. Without a chance to catch a breath, and in a single moment, I was thrust into what seemed like the deep end of identity confusion. Yes, Lily was legally old enough to make this decision, but she was my youngest, and I was heartbroken.

Transgenderism had never entered my mind. In fact, Lily consistently reflected the essence of traditional femininity, always adding a tutu to kick an outfit up a notch. Maybe if I had seen clues I could have mentally prepared. But I hadn't, and disorientation descended on me like a cold, thick fog.

I became haunted by thoughts of where I went wrong and what I could have done differently. Family and friends (the few who knew) were aghast. Of course, I was concerned for Lily's spiritual well-being, but I was also riddled with horror over what the often harsh Christian culture would say or think. This in itself should have been a red flag pointing to my own identity confused issues, but I was too busy spiraling to make the connection.

Lily, who was an illustrator at the time, drew all kinds of fascinating character reproductions from popular Disney and Pixar movies. Her work sold generously at comic conventions. One year while we were walking to her booth, Lily and I encountered a group of Christians picketing the gay vending participants. They were marching, carrying signs with anti-gay slogans. "It's things like this that make the LGBTQ+ community think God hates them," Lily sharply remarked.

I could tell Lily, who had been bullied growing up, was disturbed by Christians spouting shaming sentiments that vilified homosexuals. Naturally, she associated this rally with bullying tactics she herself had suffered in the Christian school she had attended. In other words, this Christian protest triggered Lily's own memories of being bullied and hated.

This was one of the reasons Lily felt a kindred spirit with the LGBTQ+ community. She often commented on how kind and accepting they were. These were her biggest fans, and she graciously welcomed them. They, in turn, swarmed her with support on social media and went out of their way to visit her at conventions.

I loved that Lily's heart leaned toward grace, and I highly valued her sentiments surrounding LGBTQ+ struggles. I encouraged this. But it never dawned on me that Lily would one day pull the plug on her own identity in order to live into another—trans.

After surviving the initial shock of my daughter's new identity revelation, my husband and I set out to learn more about the phenomenon of transgenderism. How does this fit into God's plans? One thing we realized was that God was allowing us to be painfully schooled in the current culture. Lily's decision gave us no choice in the matter. Because of our great love for her, we were completely vested. So, putting one foot in front of the other, we began walking (sometimes crawling) and moving forward into the uncharted territory that lay before us.

UNCHARTED TERRITORY

We had lots of tearful conversations with Lily. The prevailing heartache on both sides seemed to boil down to perspective. Ultimately, while Lily was exploring "identity" and wanted to be respected in this pursuit, we were discovering with greater clarity who we were in Christ, and we needed to have that respected as well. Gender explorers don't want family members trying to convert them back to their former selves. Likewise, Christian family members do not want to be converted away from their sacred belief system. The natural response on each side is to dig heels deeply into one's own convictions, which often turns to heated debates and eventual alienation. For this reason, from this point on, out of respect, I will address my adult trans-identifying child as Bobby, her chosen new name (unless referring to pre-trans identification. At these few times I will use the pronouns "she" and "her").

We began to realize that both sides required a learning curve of grace. When we paused and listened, we gained a great deal of knowledge about the LGBTQ+ community, and about Bobby. This created a safe environment for Bobby to not only share concerns, but also to hear ours.

Fear has the opposite effect. It shuts down communication and drives Christians to take hard lines in attempts at rescue. For example, a friend sent Bobby a note with Bible verses citing sexual sins, and at the end added that she could no longer associate with Bobby.

This person shared with me privately her hope that this biblical directive, found in 1 Corinthians 5:11, would bring Bobby to her senses:

> I am writing you that you must not associate with anyone who claims to be a brother or sister but is sexually immoral or greedy, or an idolater or slanderer, a drunkard or a swindler. Do not even eat with such a person.

The problem is that our interpretation of this verse often lacks mercy and compassion for circumstantial, mental, or emotional factors that might be associated with gender dysphoria. It leaves little room to consider that God may be entrusting us with something we don't fully understand.

While respecting other people's convictions, I desired to reach out to Bobby from a different place. I had to go with my gut on this. God helped me by leading me to Matthew 12:11 – 12. This passage describes how the Jewish religious leaders scolded Jesus for breaking the law by healing on the sabbath. They used one of God's own rules against Jesus. They didn't understand that the sabbath was created to serve mankind, not the other way around (see Mark 2:27). Jesus said,

> If any of you has a sheep and it falls into a pit on the Sabbath, will you not take hold of it and lift it out? How much more valuable is a person than a sheep! Therefore, it is lawful to do good on the Sabbath.

I love this insight into the heart of God: It is lawful to do good! In other words, it is always right to do spiritual good, even when it goes against religious ordinances. *Good* in this context is important to understand. Strong's dictionary uses the word *recover* in describing it. There is a sense of spiritual rescue. It is qualitatively different than the law. Infused with mercy and grace, it has the power to heal a person inwardly, whereas the law only addresses behavior.

Elsewhere in the Gospel, Jesus referred to Himself as the *Good* Shepherd (see John 10:14). His interest in spiritual recovery of His lost sheep defied religious customs. In other words, while the religious leaders counted up people's offenses, Jesus was thinking about rescue.

This was a game changer for me. I have a choice, even when it appears like breaking the rules of religious protocol. For me, doing good is choosing to look at this dilemma through eyes of mercy and grace rather than dogmatism. This passage showing Jesus' unconventional teachings was a life-preserver thrown directly into my deep waters of anguish. I was grateful.

The symbolism of Jesus' reference to pulling a fallen sheep out of a *pit* gave me further insight. A pit was often a hole or cistern dug by humans. In every era, the world digs cisterns of secular philosophies—wells of thought that promise us clearer understanding of who we are. Unfortunately, it is often the self-righteous religious culture that inadvertently drives people toward these humanistic answers for the meaning of existence. Hateful sentiments (like the picket signs mentioned earlier) serve to incite, arouse, and spark into flames alternative ideologies to religion. This was the case for Bobby.

Bobby was a part of a generation wounded by Church. Hypocrisy filled the unhallowed halls where Bobby grew up. In the three consecutive churches we attended, all three pastors ended up having affairs, which left the congregation reeling. Bobby's Christian school experience was fraught with bullying, which extended to the faculty.

For instance, one of the principals scolded Bobby for a minor infraction telling her she was from the devil. Children don't forget words like these that come from the lips of their spiritual leaders. Bobby lost respect for Church leadership and was deeply wounded by the bullying at her school. By the time we pulled Bobby out of this school environment and got her into yet another church, Bobby had already begun looking to the world for meaning—primarily to social media, where there were all sorts of enticing friendships and progressive ideas. Bobby found a great sense of community outside the church in secular formations of thought and philosophies.

Subsequently, Bobby embarked upon the process of deconstructing her religious tradition. "Deconstruction" among other things, means the toppling of constructs within a belief system. Many young adults raised in Christian families are emancipating themselves, not from God, but from the religious expectations of their individual upbringings, cultures, families, denominations, and theologies.

A WORLD DESPERATE FOR MEANING

One of the biggest realizations my husband and I had is that this is not just about our Bobby; it's about an entire emerging culture and generation. We live in a world desperate for meaning and wary of religious hypocrisy. But how can we connect to the lives of others who might be facing serious identity challenges when we haven't examined our own duplicity as Christians? Surely we must look inward and own up to our own confusion before we can understand identity issues others may be going through. Perhaps it's time for some deconstruction of our own.

Unfortunately, deconstruction does not come naturally to Christians. We almost compulsively build white picket fences around our lives. We represent God—and ourselves—in highly polished ways, but underneath we often harbor judgment for anyone who disagrees with our ideologies, whether in politics, personal conviction, or theology. It's not surprising that when Jesus walked the earth, He faced a lot of religious leaders wagging their fingers at Him. He continually reminded them, "It is not the healthy who need a doctor, but the sick" (Luke 5:31).

Of course, the religious leaders of Jesus' day had very specific ideas about what the Messiah would be and do. But Jesus was not interested in overthrowing the oppressive Roman government as they hoped, or counting people's offenses against them. His kingdom was not politically motivated, or (as we find in our time) celebrity-driven.

Today's Christian culture prides itself on well-organized ministries, comfortable coffee shops, and political affiliations. But true ministry is often unorganized, messy, and lacking amenities. There are no formulas, nor should there be, lest we fall into canned religiosity rather than personal, life-giving faith. As soon as we think we have a handle on successful religious protocol, the next generation proves us frauds with its new set of challenges. And it's silly to long for the old days when Christianity was simpler, because was it? Was it really? Consider how much blood was spilled just in translating the Bible in the sixteenth century!

IT'S NOT YOU; IT'S ME

In sorting out my feelings about Bobby, I felt drawn to the book of Hosea in the Bible. This book tells the story of a prophet whom God directed to marry an unfaithful woman. But before you assume that I am comparing loving an unfaithful spouse to loving Bobby, I must stop you. God did not bring me to Hosea so I could lick my wounds with the devoted old prophet. He brought me to Hosea to uncover that I am the unfaithful spouse—not Bobby. This is the reason I decided to put pen to paper and write this book. God was about to show me something that would reshape my Christian worldview. And it would be so unconventional that it might even prompt a flurry of finger-wagging in my direction.

Each chapter in this book includes verses and narratives from Hosea. As we take a deep look into areas of unfaithfulness within the Christian culture, sometimes it will be Gomer and other times Hosea who will give us insight.

What intrigued me most about the book of Hosea was *why* God would ask Hosea to do such a thing—marry a prostitute. Surely, the religious circles of that day would have raised eyebrows. We don't expect anyone—let alone a religious leader—to knowingly marry an unfaithful spouse. But God had His reasons for asking Hosea to do so, and they were poignant.

This becomes evident in Hosea 1:2, where God instructs Hosea, "Go, marry a promiscuous woman and have children with her, for like an adulterous wife this land is guilty of unfaithfulness to the Lord." God was comparing the adulterous wife to *the land*—His own people. He asked Hosea to live out on a small scale what God faced on a large scale. God was inviting him to a deeper understanding of what God Himself felt in being committed no matter what. He was giving Hosea a glimpse of His personal agony from a divine perspective. But even more than this, it was a sacred life-lesson on the very nature of God's love and what it looks like applied. It was, indeed, a glimpse of the gospel.

We read about this in hindsight and embrace this strange story without hesitation. Hosea's contemporaries, however, must have been confused. We forget how scandalous this must have seemed to the religious minded. I'm sure they could have created clever picket signs about what Hosea was doing wrong. But then they would have missed out on the purpose of God's assignment for him—underneath all their broken rules.

Against this backdrop, as I work through the complexities of identity confusion, I see an opportunity. What does God want me to experience when it comes to understanding issues of identity? What is the bigger purpose underneath the broken rules of my theology? Is He allowing Bobby to show me? I believe He is.

Our Christian culture's identity does not reflect who God really is, and the Bobbys of the world are inevitably misled by this. This was a pivotal realization for me. God's love is generous, sacrificial, and unconditional, yet we often veil this beautiful reality with representations that don't look like God at all. This is why we must get at the root of our own muddled Christian identity and recognize the effect it has on the lost and confused world.

Here is what I mean. The world today is responding to God based on Christians' often bogus portrayal of Him. This is where Hosea's experience comes in. God asked Hosea to be the picture of God's committed love regardless of an unfaithful bride, and Hosea faithfully committed himself to represent God's love well. That's what we are also called to do, there is no greater responsibility. Instead, too often we expect others to commit themselves to a God we have represented as fickle, shallow, scornful, two-faced, immature, and judgmental—like us.

Somehow, I just can't imagine Jesus holding a hateful picket sign.

So here's the question we need to ask ourselves: Is my representation of Christ clashing with His true identity and nature? Do we, as Christians, look like the One to whom we are to be conformed in likeness? As Scripture reminds us, "For those God foreknew He also predestined to be conformed to the image of His Son" (Romans 8:29).

What does this look like for me? What doesn't it look like? Let's explore further.

CHAPTER 2

BACK TO THE BEGINNING

I was having a hard time adjusting to the magnitude of Bobby's new direction. My heart volleyed between grief and confusion. The ambiguous nature of it all felt confusing, and I needed clarity.

What was this current trans movement about? There were terms and ideas I had never heard of before. Thankfully, I came across a thoughtful and investigative book on the subject. In this book, *Irreversible Damage: The Transgender Craze Seducing Our Daughters*, author Abigail Shier shares conversations with psychologists and medical doctors. Her interviews revealed the alarming trend of treating prepubescent identity confusion with puberty blockers. The writer, concerned over children's inability to fully comprehend potential consequences, lobbied for greater responsibility from attending adults.

To further demonstrate her point, the author shared the story of a child Holocaust survivor she had learned about at the Los Angeles Museum of Holocaust and Shoah Foundation. She explains how the girl's parents paid a Catholic family to secretly take their daughter and pretend she was their own. The girl was given a Catholic name, rosary beads, and immersed in new culture. In the blink of an eye, the child's Jewishness was blotted out by the adults in whose care she was placed. After the war the girl, who was now an adult, felt entirely disconnected from her Jewish roots. The author, who considers heritage essential to identity, was saddened that the child's background was so suddenly expunged. She compared this story to adolescent girls today who lose their identities by rashly transitioning into boys.

I could tell this analogy held strong personal sentiment to the author. And her argument that adults carry real responsibility to the children in their care is compelling. But her comparison of identity significance did not go back far enough for me.

Let me explain. If the progressive line of thinking in our postmodern times is that people are not bound by gender, then parallel logic must be applied to history and ethnicity. In other words, the same argument that we cannot be limited by gender for understanding who we are as humans must apply to our ancestral origins as well. Ancestry can be no more of an answer than physiology. Abigail Shier's thoughts, although provoking, were rooted in the identity she believed paramount. This is the same way proponents of gender confusion today argue their case. In both cases, *identity* is seen as preferential and personal.

IDENTITY FROM A DIFFERENT ANGLE

This got me thinking about what identity *isn't*. I can't help wondering if all the shifting and ungluing of identity constructs happening in the world is simply bringing to light what we are not. In fact, it might surprise you to know that Scripture supports a more progressive view of identity in terms of *what it is not*: "There is neither Jew nor Gentile, neither slave nor free, nor is there male and female, for you are one in Christ" (Galatians 3:28).

In this verse, common identifiers like nationality, social position, and gender are neutralized. This tells us that answers to the deep questions of identity must come from a higher place. We'll touch on the phrase "in Christ" in the following chapter. But for now, let's continue our exploration of what identity is not. To do this, we need to go all the way back to the beginning. Consider this: every kind of genealogical, ancestral, and physiological make-up in the world originates from Adam and Eve. They are the original human template designed for fellowship with God, spiritual connectivity intact. We read in Genesis that God said, "Let us make mankind in our image, in our likeness..." (Genesis 1:26).

The Bible is not talking here about likeness of flesh and blood, since God is spirit, but rather likeness to the unseen image of the Creator—a kindred sameness of spirit. Our bodies are simply tents made of dust that house these spirits.

It was only after the fall that diverse cultures emerged. Humans headed different directions, creating languages, customs, and distinctions between people. The only thing they had in common was spiritual separation from God, and this is where identity confusion first surfaced on the timeline of history. It was not diversity that caused confusion among people, but rather identities separated from God. Our original identity was meant to be connected to God, so we might even say that any disconnect from God is an alternative identity to the one we were given originally.

Stay with me on this point for a moment. In my opinion, our greatest concern cannot be to restore our children to their birth identity. Why? Because even that falls short of our truest identity, which was always meant to be located in spiritual communion and fellowship with God our Creator. Through Adam and Eve's fall, all of humanity became spiritual orphans. Each one of us is now born into lost and confused identities and subcultures *separated* from God.

In other words, identity confusion is nothing new. We simply may not have recognized it for what it is.

IDENTITY CONFUSION IS NOT NEW

Subcultures have always been a reality throughout history. The trans community today is simply one of many. Christians get offended by the normalcy it receives, forgetting the same societal adaption can be said of any culture, past or present. Think about the practice of voluntary castration in the early Christian era for religious dedication, or venerated leaders of religion receiving lofty titles, even after Jesus taught His followers not to call anyone "rabbi" or "father" (see Matthew 23:8 – 9).

Or go back even further to the common tradition of having multiple concubines. In the Old Testament, King David, the man after God's own heart, had several; his son Solomon had 300. As peculiar as these traditions may be to us (or even offensive), they were each accepted customs in their season. All this to say, no matter what the culture is, God is not shocked.

In our times, advanced technology makes preferential sexual identification, and the procedures to enhance it, a viable reality. Again, God is not shocked!

THE VERY FIRST CASE OF IDENTITY CONFUSION

This is why it's important to get past our own shock at people's outward presentation and take a look inward to the soul. Satan, who is the culprit behind identity confusion, is perpetually trying to lure us into creative (and personalized) forms of identity apart from God. In Genesis 3:1 – 7, we see Satan's pitch to Eve:

> Now the serpent was more crafty than any of the wild animals the Lord God had made. He said to the woman, "Did God really say, 'You must not eat from any tree in the garden'?" The woman said to the serpent, "We may eat fruit from the trees in the garden, but God did say, 'You must not eat fruit from the tree that is in the middle of the garden, and you must not touch it, or you will die.'" "You will not certainly die," the serpent said to the woman. "For God knows that when you eat from it your eyes will be opened, and you will be like God, knowing good and evil." When the woman saw that the fruit of the tree was good for food and pleasing to the eye, and also desirable for gaining wisdom, she took some and ate it. She also gave some to her husband, who was with her, and he ate it. Then the eyes of both of them were opened, and they realized they were naked; so they sewed fig leaves together and made coverings for themselves.

Satan had persuaded Eve that once her eyes were opened, she would know what was best and what would feel right. She would experience a *wokeness* and could be true to herself in this awakened condition. We see this enticing alternative laid out before her: *For God knows that when you eat from it your eyes will be opened, and you will be like God.*

To receive God-like wisdom and be master of her own destiny sounded good to Eve. Satan convinced her of a narrative that felt empowering. But as right as it felt, it brought immediate death (spiritually speaking) and separation from God. Satan is peddling the same narrative to us thousands of years later. Just as he did with Adam and Eve, he wants us to believe that we can master our own identities. And to be honest, on a secular level, apart from the Spirit's influence, nothing feels more right.

Our loved ones who are shaping their identities to suit their preference believe and embrace this *human mastery* with every fiber of their being. They are breaking from what society, especially the hypocritically religious, tells them they need to be and deciding for themselves who they believe they are. They view all rejection of their assumed identity as a blanket rejection of themselves. This ideology is fortified by their community, which is often much more affirming and generous then the Christian culture—and feels safer.

When my husband and I moved to our new home in the country, we began our search for a local church. While not making it known that we were parents of a transgender identifying person, we were met over and over again with unfriendly voices toward the LGBTQ+ community, as well as antiquated ideas about womanhood. These sentiments dogged us at every turn. We longed to be part of a church that would love us through this trial and pray for our Bobby with us. But we couldn't find one we felt safe in.

The problem with many churches is that they are suffering the same malady of wanting to master their own identities. Veering from the centrality of gospel they emphasize preferred doctrinal choices. Theological and intellectual leanings become paramount, and to be honest, nothing feels more right to the studious conservative evangelical. For them, identity preference is found in their credo affiliation. Objections to these ideals are often interpreted as blanket rejections of themselves and God.

I parallel these two patterns, not for the purpose of putting either one of them down, but rather to highlight that identity confusion is identity confusion, whether it's found in the church or in the world.

REFLECTING JESUS

In the forthcoming chapters, it may at times read as if I am abandoning Christian values, but I am not. I'm simply stepping out of theological dogma to seek the heart of Jesus—and it feels wonderfully refreshing. If there is one thing Bobby's journey has taught me, it's to be much more purposeful in identifying with Jesus, rather than church culture. I will do my best to share my thoughts from this perspective, not as an expert, but as a mom.

Our journey starts by taking a good hard look at our own defective religious constructs. The identity we lean into as Christians is critical if we want to be vessels of mercy to those who are identity confused. Notice the process we are called to in Matthew 7:5, "First take the plank out of your own eye, and then you will see clearly to remove the speck from your brother's eye."

Then you will see clearly.

Then and not beforehand. *Then*, after what was said previously has been completed: *taking the plank out of your own eye.*

The words *see clearly* are translated from the Greek *diabepo* and, according to Thayer's Greek Lexicon, can be interpreted as a blind person recovering sight. In other words, we are all blind to some extent, trying to make sense of life and identity through broken lenses. As Christians we immediately gravitate toward religious rules, interpretations, and traditions, as well as preferences and prejudices, when evaluating things we don't understand—which further evidences our blindness.

Romans 2:1 highlights this problem within the church. Paul warns that those who self-righteously pass judgment on others are condemning themselves: "For at whatever point you judge another, you are condemning yourself." The fact is that legalism is its own deadly kind of subculture, and the New Testament warns about this over and over. This is because legalism leads broken people (of all cultures) to the law—which condemns. God's grace through Christ, however, rescues. That's why Paul writes, "I do not treat the grace of God as meaningless. For if keeping the law could make us right with God, then there was no need for Christ to die" (Galatians 2:21).

Only when we take steps to remove the planks of self-righteousness from our own eyes can we see through the eyes of mercy and grace like our heavenly Father. Removing the plank is not a qualifying step, but rather an enabling one. There is a difference.

In other words, we don't engage in the process of removing the planks from our own eyes simply to be qualified judges of others; that would be to miss the whole point. Instead, removing the planks from our eyes allows us to move forward in searching our own heart, trusting that the result, although painful, can bring wisdom, insight, and blessing to others.

Spiritual sight is a gift—not just for us, but for others. Oftentimes, we don't receive this gift unless suffering is involved. I recently was contacted by a woman I knew from church but had not seen in many years. She was always very proper and put together. *Why was she reaching out to me?* I wondered. Maybe she had heard about Bobby and wanted to update me on the latest Christian political movements against the LGBTQ+ community. That certainly was not out of the realm of possibility, since I'd already been contacted with petitions and pamphlets from Christians who found out about Bobby's direction.

Maybe a lecture on failure to raise a godly child was in store. I waited. The next day I decided to text instead of call—texting was safer.

The response I received was a surprising blessing. Oh, how my heart needed it, too. *God knows.* The text read: "I heard that Bobby has lost her way. I wanted to encourage you, I know the ache of loving a prodigal. Just wanted to share some hope."

There it was—the gift of hope-filled vision. In truth, it might be more accurate to say Church culture has lost its way. Still, it was an offering of encouragement, forged by pain, no planks or logs in sight. How marvelous!

This is what was happening in Hosea's life. God allowed Hosea to experience the same suffering with Gomer that He experienced with Israel. This gave Hosea an *enabling* of introspection—clarity amidst confusion. Whatever planks may have been present in Hosea's heart during this strange trial gave way to sacred perspective. In this vulnerable, humble space, Hosea was able to view Gomer through the lens of God's heart. Hosea's heart was being fashioned into the likeness of the Savior to come.

This in turn allowed Gomer to experience the kind of love rooted in God's identity, not Hosea's (or her own). Hosea became an image bearer of God's unconditional love. It was not love based on legalism, selfishness, or misplaced righteous zeal, but deeply steeped in Covenant Promise.

In the next chapter, I will share how God clarified this for me during a confusing and tense dialogue with Bobby. What could have been a crushing debate ended up revealing that my love needed to reflect God's image (not Christian culture). And it would be *this* reflection, not my own, that would be able to cast transformative light into someone else's life.

CHAPTER 3
A NEW DESIGN

We sat eye to eye across from each other in the outdated library. A disco ball set on top of a bookcase reminded me of the glitzy pop culture of the '70s. Our seats, half-moon shapes that swiveled, were six feet apart. But even this whimsical setting did not detract from the fact that we were about to engage in serious conversation.

Bobby was notably stoic. I had seen this posture many times. Bobby is blessed with high intelligence and a mind ready for battle. Likewise, Bobby recognized my posture—ready to strike with moral conscience. So there we sat, eyes locking.

In this moment of silence, I experienced a wide range of emotions.

My family jokes that my "eye contact" feels like a kind of elongated death ray. They sweat it out, hoping I will say something—anything—to get past *the look*. Meanwhile, absorbed in thought, I simply stare. And on this day my silence lingered under the weight of the subject matter.

Finally, I asked, "Honey, if you were sitting with Jesus and you told Him you wanted to be a boy instead of a girl, how do you think He would respond?"

Literally without blinking Bobby replied, "He would tell me He loved 'me' the person inside, my soul, and that in the end there would be no gender, and none of this would matter."

Honestly, I was caught off-guard by this answer. Bobby's words revealed something about my own heart that I didn't see coming. Did I think God was unable to love someone I judged as stepping outside of His design? For that matter, at what point do any of our departures from God's design qualify us to no longer be acceptable to Him? Remember our comparison in the last chapter of David and his concubines?

My mind raced through some verses in Matthew chapter 5. In this passage, Jesus' reorienting words remind us that everyone is "guilty" of veering from God's original design in one way or another.

In verses 21 to 23, Jesus states the obvious—and then realigns with the not so obvious:

> You have heard that it was said to the people long ago, "You shall not murder, and anyone who murders will be subject to judgment." But I tell you that anyone who is angry with a brother or sister, will be subject to judgment. Again, anyone who says to a brother or sister, "Raca," is answerable to the court. And anyone who says, "You fool!" will be in danger of the fire of hell.

In this verse the obvious departure from God's design is murder—the not so obvious is the inflamed response "You fool!" Interestingly, Jesus puts them in the same category.

Verses 27 and 28 continue this theme: "You have heard that it was said, 'You shall not commit adultery.' But I tell you that anyone who looks at a woman lustfully has already committed adultery with her in his heart." In these verses the obvious departure from God's design is adultery—the not so obvious is looking at someone lustfully. Jesus is saying that they both hold equal weight.

FAILED LOGIC

As I continued in this line of thought, I reasoned, *Sure, we all mess up, but then we get back on track.* Bobby's direction seemed different to me; it was long-term. In my opinion Bobby was making a conscious choice to live in a continuous state against God's design *and believe it's okay.* That's when the next two verses (31 and 32) hit me:

> It has been said, "Anyone who divorces his wife must give her a certificate of divorce." But I tell you that anyone who divorces his wife, except for sexual immorality, makes her the victim of adultery, and anyone who marries a divorced woman commits adultery.

I am this person! My husband is this person! I was married before—twice. My current husband married me anyway. And we are choosing to be married and stay married *and believe it's okay.* So, in essence, according to this verse, we are making a conscious choice to live in a continuous state against God's design. What does God think of this? Do Bobby's words have merit for my conundrum? Do I get to pick and choose what's an acceptable departure from God's design? What about God? When He looks at me, does He see only a continuous state of adultery?

I was reminded, once again, of the warning in Romans 2:1, "For whatever point you judge another, you are condemning yourself."

My own judgment of Bobby fell back on me, and I'm so glad it did. God used this passage to reaffirm that security in Him is not about rule-keeping or working our way back to an original design. In fact, as fallen humans, we are shaped and formed by more design variations then we could ever possibly imagine.

Back to my own straying from design. A few chapters later, in Matthew 19:8, Jesus actually addresses the predicament of divorce. This not only helped me understand why divorce was permitted, it gave me insight into all forms of departure from God's original design. Look at the words: "Jesus replied, 'Moses permitted divorce only as a concession to your hard hearts, but it was not what God had originally intended'" (NLT).

Notice this verse does not abdicate original design. This is an important point. It reminds me that God's design is perfect, flawless, and never-changing. So why the *concession*?

We find our answer embedded in the word *hard*. *Hard* in the Greek is *sklerokardia*. Strong's dictionary defines it as "destitute of spiritual perception." This explains why all of us (being destitute of spiritual perception at some point and on some level) are permitted *concession*—a straying from God's original design.

Certainly, God's original plans remain the immutable design of creation, but straying is an inescapable result of brokenness this side of heaven. In other words, movement outside of original design is the linear byproduct of the fall across the timeline of history.

The word *concession* gives us further insight. Strong's dictionary uses the words *allow*, *permit*, and *suffer* in describing concession. It means not only permitting the action, but the suffering that coincides. This is significant. In fact, the King James translation uses the word *suffer* in place of *concession*. This means any straying from original design will be causatum, which means to have an effect, or have inevitable consequence. Causatum is a natural outworking of concession. When concession occurs, simultaneous suffering follows; they are inseparable. We will always suffer when we move outside God's design in ways that accompany that particular movement.

For instance, suffering is easily traced in divorced scenarios. Children of divorce hurt and feel divided. They wonder if it's their fault. They often struggle later in life with insecurity. There is loss involved, and suffering is inescapable. Even though a divorced person may enter a new season that is filled with happiness, it does not negate the suffering that coincides in some form.

Another example might be things we should do but don't. The theological term for this is *sin of omission*. James 4:17 says, "If anyone knows the good they ought to do and doesn't do it, it is sin for them." For instance, when we don't reach out to someone in need because were too busy with our own agenda, the concession of not reaching out comes from *hardness heart*. The causatum would be suffering on their end. We might never see or feel the effect ourselves, but there is still suffering involved.

Concession is a difficult concept for the Christian culture to embrace because it involves rule-breaking, and rule-breaking infuriates the religious-minded. But the truth is that we are free to make our own choices in this life. Those choices, however, will be a direct product of varying levels of hardness of heart and carry corresponding consequences. Even those choices made by others before we were born will have a causatum effect on our future.

Consider a fatherless child birthed from a mother on drugs. That child's future, through no fault of their own, will suffer the causative consequences of someone else's choices.

Even though we are free to make our own choices in this life, some of those choices will automatically carry repercussions, pain, and heartache for us and others. 1 Corinthians 10:23 underscores this: "'I have the right to do anything' you say—but not everything is beneficial. 'I have the right to do anything'—but not everything is constructive."

Looking back at Bobby's answer to my question at the beginning of this chapter, I recognize a great confidence many Christians lack: "He would tell me He loved 'me' the person inside, my soul, and that in the end there would be no gender, and none of this would matter." But at the same time, I can see the causatum reality of the words *in the end*. There is a lot of life for Bobby between now and the end. The days, months, and years of Bobby's life are important to God— not only *the end*. God sees Bobby relationally as His child, not just a soul that makes it into heaven. There is a specific design for Bobby's heart in connecting to God while on earth.

For instance, at age eleven, Bobby, being unusually capable of communicating with adults, was invited into a training seminar for children's evangelism at our church. When the class was over, Bobby announced with great joy, "I know what I am supposed do with my life." She was on fire. She got it—the passion of the Gospel and the important role it would play in her life and the lives of others. I remember praying that Bobby's art would be a part of this calling, like C. S. Lewis, whose mystical story-telling abilities brought the kingdom of God to life in the imagination of millions.

This kind of life experience, and many others, incorporate the space between *now* and *the end* for all of us. The choices we make in this in-between time will be a direct result of concessions of the heart. Furthermore, those concession of heart will have a direct impact on our affections for God.

BECOMING AWARE OF OUR OWN CONCESSIONS

Matthew 5 makes it clear that we all have movement outside God's design. Becoming aware of our own concessions not only changes how we view others; it helps us to realign our own priorities in this life.

Perhaps this is what happened to the religious leaders who tried to trap Jesus. They wanted to see if He would sanction the stoning of the adulterous woman in John 8. They viewed themselves as righteous (rule-keepers), and the woman as unrighteous (a rule-breaker). And because they thought Jesus a "compromiser" of their righteousness, they set out to trap Him with a sure bet— "the rules." They even put the law of Moses squarely under His nose. "The law of Moses commanded us to stone such a woman. Now what do you say?" (Matthew 5:5)

But the unexpected unfolded. Jesus wrote something in the sand, and it caused them to drop the rocks from their clenched fists. I can almost hear a symphony of stones hitting the ground. It is as if somehow in that moment, they were divinely made aware of their own concessions. Jesus spoke these powerful words: "Let any one of you who is without sin be the first to throw a stone" (v. 7).

What a picture!

Bobby's journey has caused me to dig deeper—in an introspective way. How do I approach God with the paths I have forged away from His design? Am I still loved by Him?

The first thing I need to grasp is that divine restoration is personal in nature, meaning it is to God, not to an original design. No one can ever live up to the perfection found in the original design. And just in case we think we can, Jesus brings the theme of Matthew 5 to a stunning climax, the final nail in the coffin: "Unless your righteousness surpasses that of the Pharisees and teachers of the law, you will certainly not enter the kingdom of heaven" (v. 20).

Jesus laid out the impossible, lest any person think themselves capable of keeping to the original design. He used the Pharisees and teachers of the law as an example. These people walked closest to God's design for morality, yet they were hypocrites. Even they fell wildly short.

NEW WAY

There is only one way to surpass pharisaical righteousness, and that's what Jesus was leading up to. It would be the grand moment in history that would change everything: complete and total rescue from our fallen natures. It would not be going backward to the original design. Remarkably, it would be stepping forward into a breathtaking *new design*.

The Abrahamic covenant pointed the way to this new design.

The laws of Moses showed unilateral human inability apart from this new design.

And now, there, standing right in front of them in the flesh, was the NEW DESIGN—Jesus—the one referred to in Jeremiah 23:6,

"This is the name by which He will be called: The Lord Our Righteous Savior."

Just thinking about it floors me! Jesus was about to turn their world upside down with a plan forged from the beginning of time—a superior design. But first He had to show them that all have strayed and fallen short of the original design. The biblical laws were given for this reason, to highlight this universal fact. "Therefore no one will be declared righteous in God's sight by the works of the law; rather, through the law we become conscious of our sins" (Romans 3:20).

Our sweet Jesus stepped in and lived that perfect design for us—the one we couldn't—dying in our place in order to redeem us. Jesus, the only person ever to live a sinless life (no concessions) passed the challenge found in Matthew 5: *Unless your righteousness surpasses that of the Pharisees and teachers of the law.* In fact, He states that He came for this purpose: "Do not think that I have come to abolish the Law or the Prophets; I have not come to abolish them but to fulfill them" (Matthew 5:17).

Jesus' fulfillment of the old (the laws) was an act of love on our behalf that made the *new* possible. When we enter into this mysterious love, we are entering into this new design (in Christ). We are operating out of His righteousness—not our own.

God sent the second Adam, Jesus, to accomplish what the first could not. "So it is written, 'The first man, Adam, became a living being.' the last Adam, a life-giving spirit" (1 Corinthians 15:45).

Forgiveness and healing of all concessions involves this new relationship—"adoption" through Christ's work on the cross. Where we once were all spiritual orphans, automatically born into an identity confused state (as noted in chapter two), we now have been adopted through faith in Jesus Christ. It is through this adoption that we are brought to life spiritually—reconciled to our true identity. "He chose us in Him before the creation of the world. ... He predestined us for adoption to sonship through Jesus Christ, in accordance with His pleasure and will" (Ephesians 1:4,5).

How amazing that we get the privilege to walk in this new design as children of God. Our adoption through Christ (in Christ) becomes our kindred relational status, no matter what our concessions. As Jesus walked among us—to lead us, heal us, and love us—so we also walk among a broken world as a reflection of His grace. We become *image bearers* of Jesus. What a difference from the image of an austere, angry God we often present to a broken world. I need this reminder in navigating my relationship with Bobby.

RELATIONAL CHANGE OF THE NEW DESIGN

Thinking about my sister Alexa reminds me of the uniqueness of relational change. If you saw the two of us together, you might raise an eyebrow—or even toss out a joke about which one of us belongs to the mailman. I am fair-haired and blue-eyed. She is dark-haired and brown-eyed with a tan complexion. When we were young we used to call each other Rose Red and Snow White, based on a fairy tale about two (very different) sisters with those names.

The mystery of our obvious physical contrast unfolds many years ago when my parents were approached by a local doctor to consider adopting a baby in need. A pregnant mother had asked this trusted doctor to find good people to adopt her baby. My parents joyfully accepted this request. All was set, and the baby was to be handed directly into my mother's arm at birth. But as the time drew closer, my mother discovered she was pregnant herself. I was born a few months after my sister's birth, and we were raised like twins.

As an adult it often crosses my mind, especially when I look at Alexa's exotic beauty, that God in His amazing and mysterious ways took two very different people, birthed by different mothers, and through concession and pain made them sisters. We might look at it this way: The original design was for two families completely unknown to each other to live in this world separately. My family would have moved to the East Coast while Alexa's mom remained on the West Coast in desperate circumstances. Yet in one moment, God changed us from complete strangers to sisters. I marvel! Adoption is such a special gift of relational transition. It changes everything!

Considering these thoughts through the lens of the book of Hosea, I can see this dramatically reflected. It's the glory of the *new* wrought in relational proximity—daughter and sonship.

Hosea pictures for us a God who no longer deals with us as master to servants (as found in the old), or king to subjects (also found in the old), but as a Father to beloved children (as promised in the new). Through the story of Hosea and his bride, Gomer, God displays nearness to all of us on a personal and *familial* level through Jesus.

This superior plan shows us something very beautiful. He is fully committed to us for the long haul—like a loving parent who never gives up, or a faithful spouse who sticks with us even when we fail, or a sibling who has our back no matter what happens.

This is my instruction map for dealing with people who are different from me. I want to represent this new design! I want my attitude toward those who, like me, fail at the original design, to be humble, loving, gentle, leading them to the Savior who loves them in a personal way. After all, it was His kindness that drew me to Himself (see Romans 2:4).

As I begin to practice viewing all human beings as creations beloved by God, I approach them with respect and personal affection as if they were my own family members—not as people unworthy of love because of their concessions.

This not only points beautifully to the new and better plan, but to a higher way. Rather than shaming people into a moral code (i.e., picket signs), we gently, patiently, and lovingly engage people who think differently than we do with the same patience and endurance God granted us.

Soon enough we will all be in a place of perfection in our heavenly destinations. But for now, we navigate (as Jesus did) through the sea of concessions and confused identities that inhabit this broken world (including our own). Like Jesus, who is all about rescue rather than counting the offenses, we must have compassion. This is the reason Jesus came, to be the *Good* Shepherd, to bear our offenses on the cross, and freely give His identity. "When He saw the crowds, He had compassion on them, because they were confused and helpless, like sheep without a shepherd" (Matthew 9:36).

But let's continue. In the next chapter we will explore how identity confusion can stray so far. We might be surprised how easily it can happen for any one of us. Yet even still, we can be confident that God is the great redeemer, even of our most outrageous concessions.

CHAPTER 4

YOU'VE GOT A FRIEND IN ME

As my cell phone began to ring, a picture appeared on the incoming display. It was Bobby. Her perfectly symmetrical face with its piercing blue eyes filled the screen. I studied the photo, which was both beautiful and masculine. Under the image was the still unfamiliar name, Bobby—so different from what I had called my youngest for twenty-two years. It felt foreign and confusing, beyond my ability grasp. Yet the ringing continued.

Finally, I picked up.

As we began conversing, simultaneous waves of dread and relief swept over me. The two feelings felt perplexing, incompatible, like syncretisic discord. I soon came to realize this strange dichotomy of emotions was a natural reaction to the opposing layers of life that had entered my reality. Let me explain.

For the purpose of this book, when I talk about layers, I am referring to unique life experiences that make up our journeys. Each layer shapes the complexity of a singular human existence.

Life layers are never the same for two people; like snowflakes, they are as original as the person. Even those who share the exact same event will process it differently. Professor James W. Kalat, in his book *Introduction to Psychology*, describes how life experiences are so vast and unpredictable that even psychology fluctuates by their complexities. The professor's entry in chapter one, under the subhead "It Depends," expresses the mysterious nature of it all:

It Depends

> Hardly anything is true about psychology of all people all the time. Almost every aspect of behavior depends on age, for example. Infants differ from children, who differ from young adults, who differ from older adults. Behavior also varies with people's genetics, health, past experiences, and whether they are currently awake or asleep. In some ways, behavior differs between males and females or from one culture to another. Some aspects depend on time of day, the temperature of the room, or how recently someone ate. How a person answers a question depends on the exact wording of the question, and who is asking the question. (Kalat, p. 3)

In other words, the makeup of who we are—the way we see ourselves, the way we see others, and how we live our lives—is influenced by differing layers of life circumstance and experience. Or, as Professor Kalat puts it, *it depends*.

I have raised five children and have watched them grow, change, and adjust to multiple layers of life. When I looked into their twinkling eyes as babies, I had no idea what was in store for them. Even their settings at birth differed from each other. For instance, they were all born at different hospitals; each entrance into the world was surrounded by a particular set of circumstances, doctors, nurses, culture, and social climate. This began their own unique journeys.

Life layers also include dispositional and temperamental wirings. These layers fuel preference and direction, which add to experience. Some people are naturally laid-back, others are assertive, yet others timid, and so on. There are also layers of trauma and tragedy, as well as exposures to mental, social, emotional, and psychological persuasions that add to the complexities.

Bobby was a human dynamo from day one, with no shortage of confidence. Bobby's vibrant personality was a source of bullying in her school years. Boys were captivated by her rare beauty but disdained her enthusiasm. Girls hated that the boys took such intense notice of Bobby. Both resulted in bullying.

These layers, and others, were a part of making up Bobby's human experience. This in turn affected my own life experience. My mama's heart ached for Bobby's trials, which moved me to write in order to work through the heartache. The book you hold in your hands is a product of these layers. You may feel connected, or you may feel offended. I can't control or predict either. How our story moves in your heart will be a result of *it depends*. Layers of life work this way, always flowing and changing by variables, connecting by circumstance, and influencing direction, all while moving through time.

CLASHING LIFE LAYERS

Fast forward to adult Bobby. Bobby was introducing a new layer that was foreign to me: transgenderism. The phone screen presentation of Bobby's incoming call was a reminder of this. Because this new layer had become a prominent part of Bobby's world, it automatically entered mine.

The strange unfamiliarity I felt when Bobby's call came in included navigating this new layer. It was a life circumstance that made me feel further away from Bobby. The voice on the other end, however, reassured me that I was still connected. The syncretistic discord I felt were these two conflicting emotions coming together—and as they coincided, they formed complicated emotional territory.

Bobby and I have always been close. But this layer of transgenderism created a distinct separation. Because of my theological values, I became limited in what I was able to affirm. Likewise, Bobby's new convictions did not allow agreement with where I stood. It put us in two opposing worldviews. Neither of us could adopt the other without sacrificing important pillars of personal belief.

When Bobby posted a "coming-out-as-transgender" statement on social media, it was met with hundreds of celebratory responses by the LGTBQ+ community. But Bobby confided that all the cheering in the world could not compare to a single affirming response from me—*which never came*. In both of our inabilities to unreservedly embrace the other's worldview, a layer formed of being alienated and connected at the same time. It was a layer of deep mutual love, but disagreement on an existential level.

FEELING FAR AWAY FROM GOD

This made me wonder about my own layers in terms of relationship with God. Might it be similar in some ways? What is the odd distance I sometimes feel from Him? Could it be my own life layers clashing with who He is? My earthly attachments, perhaps? My lack of faith? How about my faulty religious assumptions?

I am grateful that Jesus navigated through painful and unfamiliar territory to connect Himself to me when He journeyed to the cross. This reminds me that I am always in His sight, even if I am unable to see Him clearly through my own life layers. Clarity begins with God's view of us, not our view of Him. Layers (like concessions) never separate us from God's love, but they do separate us from a sense of closeness and affection for Him.

Thankfully, God defies the *it depends* category, reigning sovereignly over it, His purposes immovable. In fact, He masterfully works all our confusing life layers together for good (see Romans 8:28).

Nevertheless, on our end, daunting layers of life can make God feel far away. David expressed his own lack of connection in Psalm 13:1,2,

> How long, Lord? Will you forget me forever?
> How long will you hide your face from me?
> How long must I wrestle with my thoughts
> and day after day have sorrow in my heart?

God was right there, but David could not feel Him because of his own pervasive layers of circumstance and thoughts, which created a sense of separation.

Perhaps you share some of these same feelings.

In my situation, I was able to identify the layer that was separating Bobby and me. It was obvious. But somehow, I could not put my finger on what was blocking me from feeling the presence of God in this trial. I felt lost.

MY OWN LAYERS

Searching for answers, I came across Matthew 13:22, "The seed falling among thorns refers to someone who hears the word, but the worries of this life and the deceitfulness of wealth choke the word, making it unfruitful."

Notice the word *choke*. This word gives a picture of what layers can do. *Choke* in the Greek is *sympnigo*. Strong's dictionary uses the phrase "to crowd" to describe it. Imagine your hands twisting a hose to keep the water from flowing. You might observe only trickles able to get through. This is because the chokehold has crowded out space where the water is supposed to move freely. The same is true of our spiritual condition. The connection that is meant to flow freely between us and God is often crowded out by life layers.

This made sense to me. I felt choked by my emotions in regard to Bobby: fear, disillusionment, disappointment, and doubt—feelings that naturally arise when facing a difficult trial. Endless rumination made me feel like I was literally being swallowed up.

Strong's dictionary explains that the word *worries* in this verse conveys the idea of "distraction—anxiety pertaining to earthly life." In other words, the greater our connectedness to the temporal, the further away our life layers will take us from affection for the spiritual.

Again, this described me! I was absolutely distracted. I could barely think of anything else. My attachment to Bobby was huge. In fact, my attachment to all my children borders on idolization. I know a lot of moms can relate. This verse was hitting home.

It doesn't stop there. Matthew 13:22 draws a line directly from *worries* and *distractions* to *the deceitfulness of wealth*. Strong's dictionary uses the word *delusion* in describing deceitfulness. This is where it gets complicated. A delusion is a deception, a false belief or opinion about the value or reality of something. In short, it is the pull of what feels absolutely right to us. This is what makes it so tricky: We are drawn to it because it convinces us.

Sure, I could focus on the delusion I thought Bobby was being drawn to. But the Bobbys of the world could say the same about Christian culture, which has its own propensity toward delusion, whether it's fake personas, money driven motives, self-aggrandizing pastors, or legalistic expectations. Christianity is a culture subject to delusion like anything else. It's disheartening to think that delusion might be shaping the ecclesiastical constructs of our lives. But the truth is that, as broken humans, we are all under varying degrees of delusion. It's part of living in a fallen world. Certainly, God is able to burn the fog away with the light of His truth, but this is a process—and it will never be completely accomplished in this lifetime. Every single one of us will struggle with some form of inability to see clearly until we come fully into the kingdom. "For now, we see only a reflection as in a mirror; then I shall see face to face. Now I know in part; then I shall know fully, even as I am fully known" (1 Corinthians 13:12).

Even practically, on a daily basis, delusions are always crouching at the door, waiting to war against the truth.

The second we think everything is out of control, we are under the momentary *delusion* that God is not sovereign.

Those times when we doubt God's ability, we are under the fleeting *delusion* that God is incapable.

When we think that maybe our problems are not important to God, we are under the passing *delusion* that God doesn't care (God who sent His own Son to save us).

When we display self-righteous or legalistic attitudes, we are under the impairing *delusion* that God's favor can be earned.

This helps me to ease up on my expectations of Christians. After all, Christians are flawed people navigating layers of brokenness their entire lives, like anyone else. The fact that there is brokenness and hypocrisy in the church makes more sense to me as I consider these things. People who say they have been wounded by the church have most likely come into contact with a double-minded Christian (which we all are to some extent).

I can't help but think about the disciples who, although they walked daily with Christ, never seemed to completely grasp His purpose. They had their own layers of life, experiences, and thoughts. Even Peter, who in one moment realized the majesty of Jesus (see Matthew 16:16) in the next tried to block His path to the cross (Matthew 16:23). No sooner had Jesus shared with His disciples that He must suffer and die than Peter took it upon himself to pull Jesus aside and rebuke Him.

It was a layer of pride that ushered in delusion. Peter's effort to override Jesus' path to the cross not only revealed an attachment to the temporal, but an over-confidence in his own abilities.

Jesus, recognizing Peter's momentary delusion, addressed him as "Satan." "Get behind me, Satan! You are a stumbling block to me;

you do not have in mind the concerns of God, but merely human concerns" (v. 23).

This may seem harsh, but in reality, it was a charitable intervention. It caused Peter to become instantly aware of both the *delusion* and whose influence was behind it—the prince of the *cares of this world*.

WEALTH AND PRIDE

But let's take a look back at the phrase in Matthew 13:22, "the deceitfulness of wealth." The word *wealth* in this sentence brings us to the apex of understanding the entire process. In fact, the passage indicates that wealth is the direct cause of delusion.

Wealth in this context does not just mean money, but anything of the world in which we place substantial value or take pride. We often convince ourselves that some things are of more worth than they really are. But this is part of the delusion, a layer that replaces the truth of what really matters with what doesn't.

For instance, in Bobby's case, I could feel myself desperately clinging to the hope that Bobby would retain female behaviors and characteristics. I didn't want to lose my little girl. My dreams were falling apart for her, and I wanted to fix it. But the amount of value I was placing on this trivial part of the hardship was keeping me from navigating the trial well. God was obviously allowing this difficult season with Bobby to expand my own heart. My pride, on the other hand, caused me to become focused on the superficial rather than the spiritual.

Pride was blinding me.

Did I really think God was not in control, or that He was unable to handle this trial? That it held no purpose? Or that I had lost God's grace?

Pride fuels the greatest of delusions. It makes us think that success is up to us. But confidence in ourselves competes with confidence in God. Notice what Scripture says about pride: "For everything in the world—the lust of the flesh, the lust of the eyes, and the pride of life—comes not from the Father but from the world" (1 John 2:16).

Strong's dictionary describes the word *pride*—*alazoneia* in Greek—as self-confidence, and the phrase *of life*—*bios* in the Greek—as the present state of existence. In other words, it deals with being confident in the temporary state of life as opposed to the spiritual. Pride is an *interrupting* life layer that automatically misjudges value.

I had always felt confident as a mother. Now, the comfort and delight of this state of existence was being taken from me. My fingers were being pried off one by one from this premium layer of my identity. God was calling me away from this pride of life. I could no longer bask in the success of motherhood; I had to hand it back to God. It was humbling, to say the least.

Recognizing pride when we face choices will always shed light on the better way. Humility helps us to see layers for what they are. It breaks through delusion like sunshine through a cloud. Remember the thick, cold fog of disorientation I mentioned feeling at the beginning of this book? It can only dissipate through humbly seeking the Lord.

I didn't want any of my delusions getting in the way of Bobby seeing the gentle humility of Christ through me. On top of this,

I was reminded that God is the perfect Father who loves Bobby even more than I do. He is the better parent. God did not want me desperately chasing after Bobby with my own mom fix-it plans. Amazingly, God was leading me to be a friend more than a mother.

HUMILITY LEADS TO FRIENDSHIP

When I consider the importance of friendship, there is no better person that comes to mind than Rosaria Champagne Butterfield. Her faith in Christ was influenced by an unlikely friendship with a pastor named Ken. In her book *The Secret Thoughts of an Unlikely Convert*, the effects of this friendship take center stage.

First, let me share a little about Rosaria. She was leagues ahead of her time when it came to the progressive thinking of the '90s. Rosaria was a proud lesbian feminist and professor at Syracuse University. Her primary field was Critical Theory—also known as postmodernism—and her specialty was Queer Theory (a postmodern form of gay and lesbian studies). Within three years at the university, she became the director of undergraduate studies. She was invited by major universities, including Harvard University, to lecture on gay and lesbian studies.

Because Rosaria was an English professor, she set out to gain a better understanding of the Bible in order to argue intelligently against the rise of the Religious Right in America. As she describes in her book *The Secret Thoughts of an Unlikely Convert*, she had been studying the Christian Right since the 1992 Republican National Convention, where Pat Robertson declared: "Feminism encourages women to leave their husbands, kill their children, practice witchcraft, destroy capitalism, and become lesbians" (pp. 6 and 7).

Rosaria was particularly offended by the shallowness of Christians themselves. In the following excerpt from *The Secret Thoughts of an Unlikely Convert*, we pick up on Rosario's sentiments that Christians are trite:

> Christians always seemed like bad thinkers to me. It seemed that they could maintain their world view only because they were sheltered from the world's problems, like material structures of poverty and violence and racism. Christians always seemed like bad readers to me too. They appeared to use the Bible in a way that Marxists would call "vulgar"—that is, common, in order to bring the Bible into every conversation to stop the conversation, not to deepen it. "the Bible says" always seemed to me like a mantra that invited everyone to put his or her brain on hold. "The Bible says" was the Big Pause before the conversation stopped. Their catch phrases and clichés were (and are) equally off-putting. "Jesus is the answer" seemed to me then and now like a tree without roots. Answers come after questions, not before. Answers answer questions in specific and pointed ways, not in sweeping generalizations. "It's such a blessing" always sounds like a violation of the Third Commandment ("Do not take the Lord's name in vain") or a Hallmark card drunk with schmaltz. It seemed to me that the only people who could genuinely be satisfied with this level of reading and thinking were people who didn't really read or think very much—about life or culture or anything. (Pp. 4 and 5)

I appreciate reading perspectives, like Rosaria's, because it gives insight into what the unbelieving world thinks about cultural Christianity. As Rosaria fittingly puts it, *it deepens the conversation.*

Yet with these kinds of thoughts about Christians, what was it that made the difference for Rosaria? How did she get past the barrier of Christian cultural triteness and hate? As Rosaria's books so wonderfully describe—it was the intentionality of friendship meeting her right where she was.

Pastor Ken had reached out to Rosaria with a kind letter asking questions on an article she had written and published in the local newspaper. He invited Rosaria over for a home-cooked meal with him and his wife, and he set out to learn where she was coming from. *He was interested in understanding the different layers of life that made up Rosaria's human experience.* He listened with great intent, never attempting to proselytize. Only when she had questions would he offer biblically applicable answers, which naturally shed light on the Gospel. One dinner turned into many, and genuine friendship began to open the tightly closed caverns of Rosaria's heart. It took several years for Rosaria to place her trust in Jesus, and countless conversations—all lovingly and humbly borne out of friendship.

Rosaria describes this experience in her own words:

> My Christian life unfolded as I was just living my life, my normal life. In the normal course of life questions emerged that exceeded my feminist worldview. Those questions sat quietly in the crevices of my mind until I met the most unlikely friend: a Christian. Had a pastor named Ken Smith not shared the gospel over and over again, not in some used-car-salesman way. But organic, spontaneous and compassionate way, those questions might still be lodged in the crevices of my mind and I might never have met the most unlikely of friends, Jesus Christ Himself. (P. 1)

JESUS MODELED FRIENDSHIP

We end this chapter with a perspective from the book of Hosea. Hosea met the challenge to pursue his unfaithful bride with humility and friendship.

Jesus certainly understood this pursuit. After all, Hosea was a foreshadowing of what Jesus' love for us would look like. But even still, the religious leaders of Jesus' time viewed Him through layers of their own deluded judgment. "Here is a glutton and a drunkard, a friend of tax collectors and sinners ..." (Matthew 11:19).

They got the last part right. Jesus, indeed, was a friend to sinners. Strong's dictionary uses the word *fond* to describe *friend*. Thayer's Greek lexicon gives an example of "being especially dear." Astonishingly, and against cultural sensibilities, people of no distinction and ill reputation were dear to Jesus.

Jesus spectacularly and purposely befriended those who were lost, confused, sick, blind, broken, and deluded. This began the divine pull of grace—the drawing of people to Himself through kindness and mercy.

There is something very endearing in the term *friend*. It is different than making someone an object of ministry. We observe this in Hosea's story. Hosea did not see Gomer as an undertaking or a disgusting project full of layers that needed removal. He took God's view of her as one dear to His heart, through the lens of the Covenant Promise: "I will lead her into the wilderness and speak tenderly to her" (Hosea 2:14). And, "I will show my love to the one called, 'Not my loved one.' I will say to those called 'Not my people,' 'You are my people'" (Hosea 2:23).

The same holds true for us. God pursues us through Jesus. He removes our filthy garments and then lovingly wraps us in the robe of His righteousness—right over all our many life layers. In one split moment, we go from "not His people" to "we are His people"—delusions and all.

Certainly, through the washing of the Word, layers begin to transform, but never with the scrub brush of condemnation. On the contrary, we are bathed with the gentle words He speaks tenderly to us, reminding us that we are, indeed, the object of His loving friendship—even amidst our deluding and conflicting life layers.

This challenges me as Christ's ambassador to take up the same charge. I think about this when facing people who seem foreign and beyond my ability to understand. Holding tightly to the cross with one hand, I reach out the other in friendship, especially as a mom to my adult children.

As Jesus befriended, so shall I; I will remember their *dearness* to Him.

CHAPTER 5

THE WAY OF ABIDING

For a season I stalked social media, trying to make sense of what was happening in Bobby's world. Since most trans people openly share their journeys, sleuthing was easy for me. I found myself zeroing in on a personalized illustration Bobby created. The scene was a male and a female facing each other, both with sad faces. It was obvious that the two young adults in this picture represented one person: Bobby. In the drawing, they were reaching out to touch each other's hands, but were actually touching a mirror that stood between them. The art revealed a sense of mysterious duplicity.

I found it compelling. As art often does, it made me consider my own story. More specifically, it caused me to consider the dual person that I am—that all Christians are. We know from Scripture that such a paradox does exist: "I do not understand what I do. For what I want to do I do not do, but what I hate I do" (Romans 7:15). The wrestling in this verse is obvious; in fact, we get the sense of a takeover in progress. Scripture explains that the new nature we receive in coming to faith clashes with the old, and the old rises up to try and take control.

Bobby's own internal tug-of-war (as depicted in the drawing) had made its way to digital color and canvas on social media. Eventually, one of the two identities represented would dominate in expression. In a situation like transgenderism, suppression of a previous identity is necessary to successfully live into the other. This why those in the transgendered community feel it necessary to declare their birth name a dead name.

The truth is that all humans battle with identity tug-of-war to some extent. We may not be aware it, but each of us chooses how we display ourselves to a watching world. Take clothing, for instance. Some people can't imagine wearing second-hand outfits. They take great pains to be identified with specific styles. Social standing and professional accomplishments are the same; people who value these things have difficulty presenting themselves apart from their titles. Homes also reflect people's self-image, as do cars. It all comes down to what we want to be our primary presentation. We are our own image managers.

Christians often seek to manage their image by appearing "spiritually together." We wear our Christianity like brands with labels (Calvinist, reformed, etc.), never letting on that we are just regular flawed people in need of God's grace. That is, unless we select brokenness as the mask to promote our identity. In either case, it's about the identity we *choose* and want to *present*, over the identity we are hiding. We keep the other version of ourselves carefully tucked away.

A well-known women's Bible teacher, Beth Moore, knows something about this conflict. Recently, Beth felt she had to break with the prevailing Christian cultural mindset and ideals regarding women. She shares publicly that for years she felt like she had to hide these feelings, keeping them carefully tucked away, in order to belong fully to the strong conservative circles in which she moved. Living into a male-dominated Christian culture suppressed this side of her. Although her ministry thrived over the years, her inner tug-of-war never left.

Eventually she felt she had no choice but to begin breaking with the patriarchal mindset in order to be true to what she believes is God's heart for women.

She was constantly taking verbal jabs from men who felt at liberty to flex authority. For instance, a well-known pastor was publicly asked by colleagues to associate a word with Beth Moore's name. The pastor chose two words: "go home." In other words, know your place. I saw a YouTube video clip of this conversation. Watching this group of men smugly scoffing, laughing, and devaluing a woman who has dedicated her life in service to the Lord left me saddened.

In response to her decision to break away from theology that is patriarchal, Beth Moore also faced an outpouring of wrath on social media. These angry words came from the mouths (or keyboards) of Christians—nasty picket signs in the form of tweets condemning her for her decision.

Although it is a difficult road, Beth has chosen to suppress the religious construct she was accustomed to, in order to live into a new one. She trusts Jesus with every fiber of her being as she travels deeper into what she recognizes is Jesus' heart toward women.

INTERNAL STRUGGLE

Most Christians, if probed, will admit to putting on a front on some level. Many excuse it as trying to be a good witness. But since it's not genuine, non-Christians are turned off by it. The truth is, often we are not doing it for their benefit anyway—we are doing it for each other. It's a type of identity one-upmanship. The harder one person tries to live into this facade, the more other Christians feel the need to ramp up their facade, and so on. One of my friends, who is married to a pastor, says it's known among male church leaders as comparing "chenis" size—the "ch" stands for Christian performance.

Obviously, this kind of behavior is far from representing Jesus—the very thing Christians truly want to do.

So what's really happening, then? It's the old nature trying to dominate. It's the internal struggle that all humans—including Christians—share, as mentioned above: *I do not understand what I do. For what I want to do I do not do, but what I hate I do.*

Maybe you have seen a comical rendition of a person with a devil on one shoulder and an angel on the other. Each seeks to influence the person's direction by appealing to their emotions. As silly as this sounds, Scripture indicates there really is an emotional pull on the heart in this tug-of-war: "No one can serve two masters. Either you will hate the one and love the other, or you will be devoted to the one and despise the other" (Matthew 6:24).

In this verse, notice the emotional word—hate—placed opposite love. Devotion is pitted against despising. These are strong opposing sentiments, certainly powerful motivators to exalt one and squash the other.

As the verse states, *no one can serve two masters*, so one master must rule. The title "master" in fact implies a singular control; there can be only one top spot. Our old nature, which is attached to temporal thinking, is perpetually wrestling for domination (supremacy and control). It continually tries to take the reins from the new nature. And when it does, breakdown naturally occurs. In other words, to the degree I allow my old nature to drive my new life, it will produce toxic forms of Christianity.

THE POWER SOURCE

Scripture makes it clear, there is only one way we can overcome the dominating force of the old nature, and that is through abiding. Abiding in the Spirit puts to death our old nature. In a sense, it dead names it. "For if you live according to the flesh, you will die; but if by the Spirit you put to death the misdeeds of the body, you will live" (Romans 8:13).

Jesus taught the critical importance of abiding. The truth is we don't actually have the ability to power up our new nature on our own. Power comes solely through abiding in Him through the Spirit. "Remain in me, as I also remain in you. No branch can bear fruit by itself; it must remain in the vine. Neither can you bear fruit unless you remain in Me" (John 15:4).

According to Strong's dictionary, the Greek word *meno*, translated as *remain*, means *abiding*, or to *dwell* or *tarry*. Those who tarry in prayer, dwell in personal fellowship, meditate upon Scripture, or are conscious of Jesus in their actions possess this kind of abiding Christianity.

Abiding is necessary for us to be genuinely led by the Spirit as Christians. We can only successfully overcome our old natures through abiding. In fact, unless we are abiding, we are unable (as the verse states) to bear fruits that accompany abiding. This is a critical and life-changing realization: Abiding is the power source.

Without abiding, we naturally default to cultural Christianity, which operates on auto pilot. It is the side of us that lives into a facade, the identity of presentation. It is also what the Bobbys of the world pick up on immediately. They find it duplicitous that we want to convince them that they have a mistaken identity, when we ourselves live self-generated shams of religiosity.

For the purpose of this chapter, when I talk about cultural Christianity, I am referring to a "non-abiding" approach to Christianity. This is the most common expression of Christianity as a practice. Most people, even well-intentioned Christians, fall into this category.

Although rhythms of protocol are important in prompting and inspiring connection with God, habits or methods themselves are not the true connection. This can get confusing, because programs can appear quite spiritual. In fact, they can look downright holy. But the truth is that any kind of religious practice empty of true abiding has the propensity to produce varying levels of toxicity.

God called this out in Isaiah 29:13 (quoted again in Matthew 15:18): "The Lord says: 'These people honor Me with their lips, but their hearts are far from Me. They worship Me in vain; their teachings are merely human rules.'" When this happens, our spiritual well-being is compromised. An agenda or presentation rooted in the old nature has taken the lead.

Let me give you some modern-day examples. Toxicity happens when:

- We use Scripture to support positions of self-interest (i.e., showing off knowledge, or promoting self or agenda)

- We use biblical passages to justify abusive or oppressive environments within our homes, workplaces, or churches

- We use Scripture or theology in any way to manipulate an outcome (i.e., to make money, cause guilt, or justify license—doing whatever we want)

- We use religious positions and language to berate others on political issues or to promote personal advancement

- We present a charade of a trouble-free life to make people think we are doing Christianity well

- We equate rule-keeping with living Christianity successfully

- We believe Scripture requires us to cultivate a doormat mentality that allows others to cross over our personal and emotional boundaries

- We allow hurtful cliches to roll off our tongues, with no true love for others behind them

These are just a few of the ways we allow non-inspired religious constructs to become the automated bubble in which we live—a facade. Not only is this hypocritical to onlookers, it goes against the very nature of Jesus. It is our own attempt to master Christianity without abiding. The results are offensive to the world, and so they should be.

WHEN LOVED ONES FEEL SAFER OUTSIDE THE CHURCH

No wonder there is such a big movement among children of Christian families to deconstruct and break away from their upbringing in the Christian culture.

Parents become broken-hearted when this happens—often without recognizing the toxicity they may have contributed to make it an environment their grown kids wanted to leave.

A year ago, I invited my sister Alexa to church. She is a Christian who was wounded by the church. I knew she had stopped going because of the influence of two religious denominations that were instrumental in her world falling apart. She and her family initially attended a hyper-conservative church. Only dresses were deemed appropriate for women, and men were the supreme authorities. When this became too oppressive for her family, they found themselves on the opposite side of the spectrum in an extremely liberal church. This church inspired casting off all legalism and restraint. Long story short, while the first wounded them with oppression, the second unleashed a cavalier atmosphere where her husband felt the freedom to leave her—and he did.

It didn't surprise me when I asked Alexa if she wanted to visit to my church that she broke out in a cold sweat and began to shake. Right before my eyes, she was exhibiting post-traumatic stress syndrome from the toxicity of her own Christian cultural experiences. Alexa confided that she felt safer watching service online.

For me, this was a wakeup call. Christian leaders, including Christians representing Christ to others (like me to Bobby), are called to a higher standard of abiding, layers and all. This is because the soul direction of another is at stake, and their emotional health lies in the balance. This is why Scripture warns, "Not many of you should be teachers, my fellow believers, because you know that we who teach will be judged more strictly" (James 3:1).

Think about Jesus and how he went into the temple and turned over the tables. He did this because religious leaders were allowing toxic forms of religiosity to dominate the agenda. Greed was mastering the protocol of the temple service. Jesus made a whip of cords and drove out the salespeople and merchandise from the temple courts. He addressed them boldly: "Get these out of here! Stop turning My Father's house into a market!" (John 2:16). And in another place Jesus says, "'My house shall be called a house of prayer,' but you are making it a den of robbers" (Matthew 21:13).

My house shall be called a house of prayer. Prayer is the abiding call of the Christian. Prayer is personal and relational—our intimate interchange with God Himself. The job of a teacher or preacher (or Christian leader of any kind) is to instruct in a way that stirs this kind of abiding in the souls of believers. All other forms of religiosity fall under the umbrella of cultural Christianity (rule-keeping) governed by the non-spiritual nature. Even excellent theology and well-orchestrated liturgy are empty of power where abiding is not present.

GOD TABERNACLES WITH US

Here is the interesting twist: God's house is no longer a building such as the temple, but our very own hearts—we in Him and He in us. "Do you not know that you yourselves are God's temple and that God's Spirit dwells in your midst?" (1 Corinthians 3:16). But now the tables Jesus overturns aren't physical but spiritual. He seeks to drive out the toxicity lodged in the temple of our hearts.

So I ask myself: If there were an artistic rendering of the tug-of-war inside my own heart—both the facade and the abiding—which would be prominent?

What about you? What would the tug-of-war look like in your heart?

This brings us to some closing thoughts from Hosea 6:2 – 3. God knew that there was only one way to change His people's heart toward Him. He needed to become the way of change Himself, thereby making it possible for us to press into Him. We see this foreshadowing of the Gospel in the following passage of Hosea:

> After two days He will revive us; on the third day He will restore us, that we may live in His presence. Let us acknowledge the Lord; let us press on to acknowledge Him. As surely as the sun rises, He will appear; He will come to us like the winter rains, like the spring rains that water the earth. (v. 2 – 3)

In these verses we get the full picture of a divine process. It is God who raises us from death to life. This new life in Christ gives us the ability to press into Him, and when we do so, we receive the refreshment our spirit, mind, and soul need.

The word *acknowledge* in the Hebrew is *yada*. Strong's dictionary gives the thought of being *intimately acquainted* and *causative*. Like concession there will be an effect, but, it will be a positive one. Instead of pain and suffering brought about by our concessions, as discussed in chapter three, our acknowledging God brings spiritual health and renewal. Our connection to the power source organically causes us to be spiritually watered. Like C. S. Lewis's depiction of Narnia escaping the reign of the White Witch, the ice begins to melt, and the sun begins to shine. This can only be experienced through the divine process of abiding. It is sacred, communing connection— the opposite of presentation or show.

I realize now more than ever the importance of diligently pressing into the abiding presence of God. I don't want to present a facade to an identity-confused world, especially to my beloved Bobby. In fact, we all would do well, as Christians, to make abiding the end goal of our faith. After all, abiding is what gives us the ability to represent God deeply to the hearts of others, in a way rules do not. In the next chapter, we will unwrap the significance the role of freedom plays in this beautiful reality.

CHAPTER 6

FREEDOM TO LOVE JESUS

Bobby's identity direction generated many deep conversations within our family, and even though the subject was difficult, communication opened opportunities for greater understanding. Insights from trusted family members became invaluable to me.

One of Bobby's sisters, Jane, has been an ardent advocate for Bobby. In a conversation, Jane expressed irritation at the Christian community for voicing harsh judgmental objections to what she believes is Bobby's right—and then claiming it's out of love. In Jane's mind these self-righteous objections were translating as hate, not love. She shared a saying from a friend: "There is nothing more hateful than the love of a Christian."

At first, I felt defensive. But I had to acknowledge the prickly reality Jane was relaying. After all, I have been on the receiving end of religious judgment and objection. I know how stinging it can feel.

When I probed further, Jane communicated an example of what she thinks love should look like. She told me of a charity that supplies clean needles to addicts on the streets of Chicago. The idea is that since they're going to be using, it would be an act of compassion to at least keep them safe from infection, etc. "Christians would never do this," she explained.

I could sense Jane's frustration. In her opinion love is often withheld from people who are thought offensive—by the people who claim to be religious. From Jane's perspective, love from the Christian culture often looks more like a stamp of approval one must earn. If you don't shape up, you don't get it.

I have to admit that Jane's enthusiasm for the mission that provides clean needles for addicts inspires me. It's a kind of action that doesn't wait for the person to change before reaching out, and that seems oddly Gospel-like.

NUTS AND BOLTS

Jane's thoughts challenged me to consider love further. What does love look like, and what doesn't it look like? I was looking for some practical nuts and bolts on the matter. One thing is for sure: It shouldn't look like "approval." Jane is right. Approval is conditional, whereas love is not. Approval says, "I'll love you if," which also means "I won't love you if." Love, however, says "I love you—no ifs."

This is why showing love *well* to people we disagree with is so important. It becomes life-giving to a person who is treated as valuable and worthy of love, even if they are on a different path than our own.

Doing this, however, requires some serious effort. Here is where the practical nuts and bolts come in. More specifically, loving well requires making room for opposing emotions and intentionally creating space for conflicting feelings.

Problems arise, however, when people do not make efforts to hold opposing sentiments simultaneously. For instance, a parent who does not express objection but only ever reassures her child may soon find the child overridden with self-destructive behaviors. On the other hand, the parent who will not reassure but only ever objects may find herself alienated from her child, especially when that child grows up. As parents, cultivating the ability to carry opposing emotions at the same time is a critical and weighty responsibility. It is a long-term investment that makes a difference and allows our children to feel loved and valued in the face of conflict.

Christians have the opportunity to do this daily as ambassadors to a broken world. We can be purposeful in holding opposing emotions for people we disagree with. It won't come easy, though, because loving someone who is objectionable to us often feels very—well— objectionable.

As I think about this in relation to Bobby, I am reminded that it's normal to have opposing feelings. We touched on this briefly in chapter 4, when I described my experience of feeling simultaneous dread and relief. I want Bobby to feel lovingly valued, but at same time I need to hold tightly to my faith ideals. In order to be in relationship with Bobby, I will have to train my heart and mind to allow both of these emotional engagements to subsist.

Recognizing their contrary nature is important. My convictions will grate like sandpaper against Bobby's convictions. There is a hardship of chafing for both of us. This requires getting comfortable with being uncomfortable in order to spend time together. I have to remind myself that it's OK to feel heartache when I'm with Bobby. Bobby, who feels the same sense of ache, has shared that it's painful to be around family on holidays. Yet both of us accept the inevitability of the discomfort so we can be together and enjoy the sweet fellowship of love that is also present. Choosing to enter into loving interaction, we also enter into the discomfort.

LOVE AND BOUNDARIES

Loving well doesn't mean we have to give up our personal boundaries. In fact, personal boundaries are important because they help us express love in healthy ways. They provide safe space for us in our interactions with others. They say, "I love you, but I can only participate in your world insofar as it doesn't go against my conscience." They also say, "I want you to participate in my world insofar as it does not disregard my personal boundaries."

Sometimes, however, when we set personal boundaries, it can feel unsettling to those who disagree with us. To them proving our love requires that we give up our boundaries. This is not only dangerous to our spiritual well-being, it necessitates understanding the distinction between boundaries and love.

In my interactions with Bobby, this was imperative. I didn't have to agree with Bobby's choices, or Bobby with mine, to be in a loving relationship. But we both needed to grant safe space for each other's separate opinions.

Here's how it works: If I say I love someone but don't agree with their line of thinking on an issue, I have created a mental and emotional boundary for my own mind where my convictions and perspectives can dwell safely. This is my space and belongs to me. Within this space I have the freedom to think my own thoughts and be my own person. I can love greatly from this place. This is because my love doesn't have to do with adopting their line of thinking or forcing them to adopt mine.

It can be tricky, though, because eagerness to display love can make us confused about setting boundaries. We mistakenly think we have to agree with things that go against our conscience in order to be accepted. Or we may feel pressured by someone else's ideas. Thinking it through helps to organize it in our minds so we're not caught off-guard. That's what I hope to help accomplish in these pages, so that no matter what kind of reception (or lack of reception) we receive, we feel steady and anchored.

I find the metaphor of yoking in 2 Corinthians 6:14 to be helpful as I navigate boundaries: "Do not be yoked together ... what fellowship can light have with darkness?"

Some people take this to mean staying away from relationships with people we disagree with. But that would mean cutting ourselves off from the kind of investments we are supposed to make in people. Can you imagine if Jesus operated this way?

Yoking is about relational end goals. To yoke in biblical times was often a way of training. For instance, a mature ox would be yoked by wooden bar around the neck to an immature ox. Relation mattered. If a donkey was yoked with an elephant, for instance, there would be chaos. Other relational end goals of yoking are seen in molding, shaping, and directing. Two oxen yoked would begin to form a singular, powerful movement. When we choose to follow Jesus, we voluntarily yoke ourselves to Him. Our faith in the Gospel is our relational sameness to Jesus. And being yoked to Him, we grow and mature as we learn from Him, heading the direction He is leading.

In a season of disagreement with another, we can support that person as a valuable human being, but at the same time be careful not to yoke ourselves in the end goal sense. In fact, our disagreement may simply be an opportunity to acknowledge opposing life directions (see 1 John 4 and 5).

HERD MENTALITY

Keeping our eyes on our end goal helps us establish our bearing when navigating identity confusion. Not doing so makes us vulnerable to being swept up into herd or mob mentality. What I mean is that it's easy to be influenced by a group that feels passionate about their direction. The Oxford Dictionary describes herd mentality as the tendency for people's behaviors to conform to those of the group to which they belong.

Being aware of our propensity to herd mentality is important. Otherwise, we may find ourselves caught up in movements for or against something without fully understanding or even agreeing with them. For example, in Bobby's situation I could join the growing sentiment of parents celebrating *the choice* of a child who has decided to become who they really think they are—trans. This seems positive in the progressive world today. Not doing so might be viewed as being an unsupportive parent by the liberal movement. Although I will always celebrate Bobby—the brilliant, creative, and loving soul that Bobby is—it's OK for me to not go along with the crowd. It's OK for me to feel concerned about *the choice*, because I am.

Or I could go the other direction of joining the growing sentiment of religious shaming and fit in nicely with conservative groups. Not doing so might be seen as losing my way. But I believe it's critical to show value and dignity toward Bobby and others like Bobby. I want Bobby to feel my love, and I believe that's what the Gospel is about.

My decision should never be an either/or situation defined by herd mentality. I am an individual with my own mind. I want to be yoked to the end goal of Jesus' love. This means that my guide must be following the path He demonstrated for us while He was on earth.

Maybe you have experienced some of the pull of herd persuasion in your own life. I found a January 2021 article in *Psychology Today* titled "The Psychology of Mob Mentality" to be insightful on the social make-up of mob and herd mentality. In this article, author Gayook Wong, MSW, lists some of the effects a mob mentality can have:

> **Deindividuation**—when people are a part of a group, they experience a loss of self-awareness.
>
> **Identity**—when people are a part of a group, they can lose their sense of individual identity.
>
> **Emotions**—being part of a group can lead to heightened emotional states, be that excitement, anger, hostility, etc.
>
> **Acceptability**—behaviors that are usually seen as unacceptable become acceptable when others in a group are seen carrying them out.
>
> **Anonymity**—people feel anonymous within a large group, which reduces their sense of responsibility and accountability.

I remember Bobby describing an experience in high school where she was being openly bullied in the school lunch room. It was so emotionally brutal and relentless that she burst into tears and ran past hundreds of watching eyes, straight into the bathroom, sobbing. No one—not one person—came to check on her, and no one spoke to her the rest of that day. Yet several years later, Bobby received a few emails of apology from students who were sorry for not reaching out during those times. The herd mentality had kept even the compassionate at bay for years.

Martin Luther King Jr. once said, "There comes a time when silence is betrayal." Silence can be very powerful when communication is necessary. In navigating identity confusion, I have found communication critical even if I make mistakes along the way. Talking through issues with kindness and respect while being real about concerns or questions is valuable—even if it takes years, like in the friendship between Pastor Ken and Rosaria Champagne Butterfield.

History has taught us that herd mentality has been a factor in many inhumane acts. Of course, the greatest example of this can be seen in the cross. The influence of a large movement was undeniable that fateful morning. The voices of the thousands of people loved on by Jesus over His three years of ministry on earth were silenced while herd mentality prevailed.

BACK TO CLEAN NEEDLES FOR ADDICTS

Finding common ground helps to open avenues of showing love. Which brings us back to the example of the charity that supplies clean needles for addicts. I certainly would want to express love for them in ways that show I care—like clean needles. And this would not go against personal boundaries or conscience for me. Yet

I would still hope for more than merely loving them in the midst of addiction. My greater desire would be for them to be free from addiction and thrive. And more completely than this, I would hope for their hearts to beat for God.

This is where Jane and I differ. Humanitarianism and social justice are the end goal for Jane, whereas my hope is for someone's heart to turn to Jesus. I believe this to be paramount—without neglecting humanitarianism.

Nevertheless, Jane and I can jointly participate in clean needles for addicts, even with different end goals. Jane's point of reaching into someone's life "regardless of change" holds critical value. This is because every stage of life requires support to get to the next. In order to get to the latter, the former is crucial. Christians need to learn how to be lovingly present in people's "former" objectionable states, even if it feels unsettling. And if a person never makes it to the latter, the former is still important. More often than not, Christians miss this.

The fact that Jesus died on the cross while we were still sinners exemplifies this reality. While we were blind, diseased of heart, lost, confused, dead to hope, and even hateful toward Him, Jesus moved on our behalf with actions of love anyway—ultimately giving His own life so we could be rescued.

For us this would be considered the *former*. He loved us before we changed, without any effort or ability of our own except to embrace His atonement and receive this loving transfer of guilt. From us—to Him. Jesus reached into our objectionableness.

Following Jesus' example will, no doubt, be uncomfortable as I described earlier. Loving those we do not agree with is naturally awkward and feels distasteful. This is why many relationships end in alienation and estrangement. And, of course, if boundaries aren't respected, separation may become necessary.

But as Christians, we can reflect Jesus' patience and care for souls to those with whom we disagree. We don't have to wait for them to change to love on them well.

CHANGE EMPOWERED BY FREEDOM

When we pressure people to change, we can cause behavioral and emotional distress, as well as feelings of condemnation, guilt, and compulsion. On the other hand, when we love people with the kind of empowering freedom I've discussed, we begin to see change that is real and meaningful.

I have experienced this difference personally. Understanding the depths of my freedom—that is, my freedom to love Jesus of my own volition—has led to the greatest and most meaningful formations of my own faith. Pursuing God from this place is different than being driven by guilt and shame. This is the kind of love He desires from us. He has no interest in compulsion, which is powerless to change us anyway. Yet sadly, we often find attempts at compulsion within church halls.

I understand Jane's heart for addicts. There is a parallel of *freedom* that applies on a secular level. For instance, an addict can feel empowered when he recognizes his freedom to change. Helping him live into this freedom sets an environment for genuine recovery.

But, if you could indulge me just a moment longer, there is yet another parallel to consider. Too many Christians have become addicted to cultural habits within Christian tribalism (and herd mentality). The first five chapters of this book highlight this propensity.

We have been enslaved in many ways to toxic forms of theology, deluded by expectations of what being a Christian looks like, and this has driven our treatment of others. I know this has been true for me.

One of the greatest gifts I have been given in my struggle with Bobby is the challenge to explore my freedom outside the bubble of cultural Christianity. It has compelled me to seek the heart of Jesus rather than my default religious protocols. I have been given a fresh realization of the freedom I have to seek God in regard to loving well (with boundaries).

My religious convictions continue to go through the crucible of self-examination. This is why I have emphasized introspection throughout this book. It's critical for all of us who call ourselves Christians. The truth is, in order to love those we disagree with well, we must first look inside our own hearts. How do we do this?

First, as we discussed in chapter 3, we must reacquaint ourselves with the new design wrought by Christ. This helps us dislodge the Pharisaism that constantly tries to take up space in our hearts.

Next, we must remind ourselves of our own propensity toward delusion. This allows us to extend the hand of friendship to others and helps us stop expecting so much from other people. We live in a broken world. Jesus knew that—that's why He came.

It's important to identify toxic Christianity in our own lives, learning to recognize faulty constructs of religion. Living this way will inspire us to participate in the lives of others, even those we disagree with, in a more conscientious, considerate, and genuine way.

Sometimes we don't realize the chains that hold us back from loving or disagreeing well are simply old thought patterns that need breaking. For me, identifying areas where I default to old ways of thinking is necessary if I want to love Bobby well. I can visualize the chains falling off as I imagine how Jesus loves Bobby.

Perhaps, you have recognized areas in your own thinking where you desire change. Be encouraged: There is freedom to do so with God's help.

In closing, consider the marvelous freedom that Hosea purchased for Gomer: "So I bought her..." (Hosea 3:2). This is symbolic of the freedom that Jesus purchased for us on the cross—the new covenant, paid in full by the blood of Jesus Christ, which grants our freedom.

Keep in mind that no matter how impossible it feels, God can be trusted. The story of Hosea helps us to face the hard reality that freedom doesn't always bring immediate results. Even in Gomer's newly purchased state of freedom, she was still a wanderer at heart. But Hosea, who kept his promise to her, continued to draw her in with patience, kindness, and gentleness. He was in sync with God's end goal. God's love is patient in its pursuit of us; it is a love so amazing that it relentlessly pursues even in the face of things that feel very objectionable.

How wonderful a road map the inspiration of Hosea has been for me. I hope it has been for you, as well. Moving forward into the last chapter, we will unpack how important it is to fight the good fight of faith, especially for the sake of our loved ones.

CHAPTER 7

FIGHTING THE GOOD FIGHT

When Bobby came out to our family as trans, a divide of convictions naturally materialized among the siblings. For a family as close as ours, this was a big deal. Bobby's sister Jane, as I mentioned previously, cheered Bobby on in this new journey. Bobby's transition came on the heels of Jane's own deconstruction process of ideologies she felt were unhealthy in the church.

Bobby and Jane's emerging worldviews caused thoughtful introspection for all of us. I was particularly challenged to take a good look at the spurious views of church culture. What were those faulty patterns of religiosity that had pushed Bobby and Jane away in the first place? In particular, I wondered if I had placed too much confidence in man-made church traditions in regard to defining womanhood.

If we think about it, only recently have women been given due respect in the life of the church. Yet sometimes even that feels begrudging, like a cultural mandate men put up with because of changing times.

In the past, society never thought to look any further than women's traditional roles—things like cleaning, crafting, cooking, decorating, performing secretarial and clerical work, etc. The highest position a woman could hope to attain in the church was head of women's ministry (and even this under the supervision of a man).

Women were automatically encouraged to marry, raise children, and be submissive to their husbands. Any veering was seen as rebellious. Sadly, some were even counseled by church leaders to stay with abusive spouses.

I've had many conversations with women who expressed feeling stuck in men's submissive arm candy ideals. They resented their bodies being treated as toys with no rights once they were married.

Besides these things, a woman was automatically presumed gay or straight based on whether or not she found another woman's body attractive or stirring. But the truth is we live in such an over-sexed and over-exposed time that we all overlap in the areas of sexual stimulus. The body is beautiful on both men and women and provoking to both.

Historically, women in the church have been made to feel like there was something wrong with them if they were loud and boisterous, or if they had strong personalities and opinions. A woman felt out of place if she was business or sports-minded. Any kind of non-feminine attribute drew disapproving glances.

How did such an unhealthy environment for women evolve in the Christian world? And had I bought into it?

You bet—and probably in ways I didn't even realize.

Being a little bit of a wild card growing up, I felt a kindred spirit with the women's liberation movement. While I didn't agree with everything, I certainly understood their push for equality. Then certain biblical verses caused guilt—you know the ones. "A woman should submit in quietness and full submission" (1 Timothy 2:11). "Women should remain silent in the churches. They are not allowed to speak, but must be in submission, as the law says. ...for it is disgraceful for a woman to speak in the church" (1Corinthians 14:34–35). These verses kept me behaving like a "good girl," especially under male leadership.

I am not blaming men. Men and women are broken alike. We as humans are affected by the fall. I've seen plenty of women rage, bully, and berate their husbands and sons. This is an important subject for another time. But for now, I simply acknowledge that the church is a formation of broken people. I have come to realize that I can't lean on man-made theology to shape my views on women. Instead, Jesus' interactions with women offer the only view on womanhood I'm interested in.

THE DARK SHADOW

In listening to Bobby and Jane over time, one word pervasively surfaced. It sounded in my mind like an alarm. I could even envision it hovering over turning points of their lives, like a dark shadow one needed to run from.

The word was *shame*.

Jane described how shame had been an unhealthy motivator in church as far back as she could remember. This caused me serious reflection. I wanted to understand it from a spiritual perspective. What was this shame and how did it work? What kind of power did it have to shape an identity, or perhaps mold a new one? Did Bobby or Jane feel shame in their early years for not measuring up to patriarchal ideals of womanhood?

To find answers, I turned, once again, all the way back to the Garden of Eden. This is where we first see the word *shame* referenced. Interestingly, it was before Adam and Eve actually experienced it: "Adam and his wife were both naked, and felt no shame" (Genesis 2:25).

The phrase *no shame* in the Hebrew is *buwsh*. Strong's dictionary describes it as "[not] feeling paleness and terror." (Paleness in this context is that sinking feeling that causes skin to drain no matter what our epidermis color.) Before the devil interfered, this is how Adam and Eve lived in relation to God: no shame. Their short existence was literally shame-free. When they ate of the tree of knowledge of good and evil, however, they were suddenly overcome with shame, consumed by paleness and terror. "At that moment their eyes were opened, and they suddenly felt shame at their nakedness. So they sowed fig leaves together and made coverings for themselves" (Genesis 3:7, NLT).

After taking the advice of the devil and eating the fruit, Adam and Eve experienced an immediate turning point of thought and emotion in their lives. Now they had a visceral experience of shame. They went from the sense that all was well, to feeling the need to hide and cover their nakedness. This mental and emotional event stemmed from a source they had just mistakenly trusted. God then asked them a question, already knowing the answer. Theologians speculate He did this to help them identify the origin of this first-time-ever sensation of shame: "Who told you that you were naked? Have you eaten from the tree that I commanded you not to eat from?" (Genesis 3:11).

I've always been curious about what the tree of the knowledge of good and evil represented, and Jane's revelation of *shame* from her past led me to dig more deeply. In researching commentaries, I came across a common theme. Scholars suggest that a human, after eating from this tree, would suddenly have the ability to evaluate everything in life by their own measure of good and evil. And these values of judgment, disconnected from God, could land anywhere between good and evil, even calling good evil and evil good.

This is the fall, where separation from God in the spiritual sense first manifested and brokenness entered the world. Identity confusion became the instant state of being for all humans. When Adam and Eve lost unblemished communion with God, they were thrust into judgments influenced by the devil. It was a devastating turning point where their spiritual covering was lifted, and they became exposed to the shaming influence of the ruler of broken thinking, the deceitful spirit of the air (see Ephesians 2:1 – 2).

Adam and Eve knew something had changed. And this change, along with the skewed ability to judge good and evil, would be passed down to every generation. The whole world from this point on would be stuck under the influence of the devil whose sinister agenda is to hold us captive in *shame*.

THE RESCUER

This became our common destiny as humans—until the Messiah. Christ Himself would reverse the curse on the world. But it would come with a price—His own blood. Reconciling us to God through faith, He would clothe us in His righteousness, cover our nakedness, and take away our shame (as talked about in chapter 3 of this book).

Hosea's relationship with Gomer was a picture of this beautiful rescue. It was also a preview of a Redeemer whom many, because of skewed judgment, wouldn't even recognize, like Gomer.

This is still our reality. We Christians are not immune to the devil's influence. He wants us to continue living into judgments that are faulty and confusing. To accomplish this, he introduces all the toxic, delusional tricks we talked about in the previous chapters.

This explains why there are so many interpretations, doctrines, denominations, and conflicting judgments concerning the Bible. If everyone is different, and all assert they are right, then all must be wrong to some degree.

I've had church leaders chide me for not adhering to what they have determined to be absolute truth. I like to remind them that other scholars believe differing interpretations to be absolute truth. So which one is right? Navigating sound doctrine is never easy. But if chiding and scolding is involved, we can be sure something is amiss. Legalism is one of the biggest disqualifiers noted in the Bible for handling the Word of God accurately.

Faulty judgment of scriptural interpretations is inevitable even for the best minds. After all, none of us is God. We can see how this makes its way into everything, including interpretations and evaluations of women.

It's clear to me why Jane used the word *shame* to describe her experience in her Christian tradition. There was a lot of shaming woven into the theology both she and Bobby were spoon-fed as children. Jane shared with me memories of Bible teachers who taught she was worthless apart from Christ. This mistaken idea is prevalent in the church. Verses taken out of context can give this impression. However, it is a theology that does not represent God at all. He made us in His image, and He highly values us, men and women, equally—so much so that He gave His Son to rescue us while we were yet sinners, just like Hosea rescued Gomer.

There is no question that we are thoughtfully made and highly treasured. Our personalities are individually woven and shaped. God joyfully crafts every detail of our being—hair color, bone structure, and even those things we would see as flaws. He is the one who designed the strong, boisterous demeanor in many little girls—and finds it delightful. I know this delight, because I had one of those little girls. Bobby was a little bit sunflower and a lot tornado. She could spin into any room with sunshine and high energy.

FOR THE SAKE OF WOMEN

For the sake of all women, we need to look at Jesus' heart for women. It's the only trustworthy view. His respectful treatment of the female gender was revolutionary in its time. He was seen as progressive. His journey on earth showed radical advocacy toward this end. Take for instance the woman at the well. His interaction with her defied all sorts of stigmas and cultural norms. After His death and resurrection, He appeared to women first, giving them the privilege of delivering the first gospel account to the male disciples (who incidentally disregarded and refused to believe them).

Jesus also understood the true value of women because He was part of the Trinity that created both man and woman in God's likeness, and both on equal footing. God gave Adam and Eve joint charge to rule over creation. It was only after the fall that the narrative changed, when broken judgment entered. The Bible describes how this breakdown would manifest itself in history: "You will desire to control your husband, but he will rule over you" (Genesis 3:16, NLT).

This narrative was never meant to be *prescriptive*, but *descriptive*. It was not the original design but part of the curse. And Jesus knew this better than anyone. When we shape our realities and theologies to this broken version, we are not living into the beauty, versatility, and potential of womanhood.

The bottom line is that any judgment that deviates from Jesus' treatment and value of women causes shame, and shame causes paleness and terror. Shame is a powerful influencer toward identity confusion.

HONESTY IN MATTERS OF FAITH

As I considered these thoughts, I began to understand Bobby and Jane's desire for freedom (as we discussed in chapter 6). They wanted to experience being drawn to God's love, but not by compulsion of guilt or shame.

But at the same time, I also realized that being honest with Bobby and Jane about where I stand in matters of faith was equally important. I can't give up profession of Jesus because of broken church culture. He is my everything, the only true hope of my soul—of everyone's soul.

Even if Christian culture displays spiritual realities erroneously, or if progressive culture creates self-oriented realities convincingly—neither will change the fact that Jesus is the only reality that matters. The truth is any reality we live into that takes us further away from

His abiding presence is not going to be beneficial. And in some cases, it will be downright dangerous.

Let me offer an analogy by sharing the story of one of my dearest friends. Vivian was an amazing single mom and Christian woman. When she got remarried, her new husband (who was a Christian) was convinced that traditional medicine was an unnecessary evil. He thought that all ailments could be healed with a healthy diet. He embraced this ideal with such fervor that he went into full-time "ministry work," coaching people to eat medicinally.

When his wife got a cancerous lump on her breast, he did not allow her to pursue traditional medicine. He assured her that it could be treated successfully with the right foods. Being a submissive wife (as was her belief tradition), my friend went along with her husband's decision for her health. He dissuaded her from communicating with anyone who tried to convince her to see a doctor, insisting it was a lack of faith.

My friend's husband's firm belief that his wife was being cured did not change the reality that she was not. In two years' time, the lump progressed into a gaping open wound in her chest. Still, he would not be moved from his assertion that even this was part of the healing process.

When she was in so much pain that it became unbearable, her son called me. I drove over immediately. As I entered her apartment, a notable aroma of decaying flesh greeted me. Death was most certainly in the air, regardless of her husband's insistence that all was well.

Knowing she was highly under the influence of a false reality, I treaded carefully. I was able to convince her to let me take her to the emergency room. Her husband was angry and refused to come. MRI scans revealed her entire body was riddled with cancer. What had started out as a small lump on her breast, which could have been surgically removed, ended up inoperable stage four cancer.

When her husband finally came to the hospital to visit her, the doctors gave him the grim prognosis. But he still would not be swayed. And to this day he insists his wife died from the medications given to her by these doctors.

What an identity confused quandary I had entered into with my two Christian friends! He was a self-appointed expert on "biblical" health. She was a submissive wife who was convinced God would want her to obey her husband. These were two lovely people, who both believed their realities whole-heartedly. Their choices, which they were free to make, bore severe repercussions.

What could be done for my dear friend at this point? What can be done for any of us when we are in a season of identity confusion? We are *all* broken and live in false realities in some way or another. Obviously, Christians are not exempt. In fact, the entire New Testament urges us *not* to continue in the flesh what was started in the Spirit. This implies that we have the tendency to default to the flesh (temporal reality). And the moment we operate out of the flesh, we become identity confused regarding our spiritual reality. In other words, if I try and speak into someone else's life from the fleshy part of my heart, my judgment is instantly skewed—even as a Christian.

What my friend needed was a reflection of Jesus. She needed people who, like Hosea, would love on her regardless of the false reality in which she was immersed. But (and this is an important *but*), she also needed people who would not take on her reality as their own. If they did, how could they help her through the process of death, or offer her hope in Jesus' mercy and grace in her few remaining weeks on earth?

By the same token, what my friend did not need was people to come into her hospital room with shaming picket signs of "I told you so" or chiding, scolding interpretations of absolute truth. She needed tender whispers of the gospel of Christ. And that is what God provided through a handful of Hoseas in her last hours.

THE SWEET AROMA OF ABIDING FAITH

I tell this story to illustrate that gently living into our faith through love often speaks in ways that logic can't. Trusting God in the midst of identity confusion conveys an unspoken theology that even some of the greatest theologians miss.

But I must caution that there is a difference between living *into* faith and living *out* faith. Living *into* faith is about my own relationship with God in a real and active sense—abiding—even when no one is watching.

Living *out* my faith is for show. It says I am manipulating whoever is watching with behaviors that look and sound spiritual to influence their choices. Incidentally, this faulty type of religiosity is very common, and it breeds shame.

When we are told to "work out" our salvation in Philippians 2:12, it does not mean acting spiritual for others to see. "Continue to work out your salvation in fear and trembling." "Fear and trembling" in this context mean trusting God's abilities rather than our own—over and over again. It's a humble, trembling dependency.

The fact is, I'll never be wise enough to debate the progressive wisdom and intellect on the subject of identity confusion (there is too much I don't know that only God knows). And I'll never be savvy enough to sway the logic of fuming Christian legalists who shame the Bobbys and Janes of the world that Christ came to rescue (same as me).

This puts me in a different space altogether, a kind of a "misfitting" with both.

Leaning into one or the other would cause me to become either immobilized or erroneously super-charged. Alternating back and forth would cause me to be passive-aggressive. And although it sometimes feels lonely to step back from both, this is where I'm supposed to be. Perhaps you feel drawn to this space also.

I am reminded of the conversation between Joshua and the angel in the Old Testament. When Joshua asked the angel who appeared on the battle scene what side he was on, the angel replied, "Neither" (Joshua 5:13 – 14). In essence, the angel was pledging his allegiance and dependence to God alone.

Clinging desperately to the Lord, I land in "neither" when it comes to choosing broken sides here on earth—especially since all sides are broken to some extent. My position is one of dependence on the Lord, putting all things in God's hands, begging for His provisions and rescue to both. We can't go back to the original design, but we can look to the *new design*—Jesus and His redemption. He presides here.

EMBRACING A MIS-FITTING RESPONSE TO THE WORLD

For this reason, I do not rise up and fight the world in my own ways, like Peter who cut off an ear of the soldier coming against Christ. His was a passive aggressive approach. I also do not respond like the disciples who asked Jesus if they should call down fire from heaven on their opponents. Jesus' response to them was telling: "You know not what manner of spirit you are of. For the Son of Man is not come to destroy lives, but to save them" (Luke 9:55 – 56, NKJ).

Instead, I remember the spirit I am of: "For God did not send His Son into the world to condemn the world, but to save the world through Him" (John 3:17). And "Mercy triumphs over judgment" (James 2:13).

Peter's impulse to cut off an ear was autonomous. He was exercising his own skewed judgment in a moment of identity confusion. He was mistakenly self-identifying as a protector of Jesus.

Jesus' response, "Put your sword back into its place" (Matthew 26:52 – 53), shows us how we are to conduct ourselves if we truly want to live into His identity. The word *back* in the Greek is *apostrepho*. Strong's dictionary uses the words *turn back* or *turn away from* to show the action of rejecting our old way. In other words, though our natural human response is to fight in one way, we are to reject the impulse for another, higher way.

Jesus then asks a question, intended to reorient their earthly attempts to fight by reminding them that with a simple breath, God could wipe everyone out: "Do you think I cannot call on My Father, and He will at once put at My disposal more than twelve legions of angels?" (v. 53).

Something else was going on—a bigger battle fought in a different way. Jesus' words reveal that it will temporarily look like He is losing. And many times, that's exactly how it will look and feel for us. In the midst of this kind of disorientation, we, like the disciples, need to be reminded who is ultimately in charge—even when it looks bleak.

The truth is I am not fighting against Bobby and Jane, or against the legalistic Christian culture. I am fighting the evil forces that have been from the beginning trying to influence and skew our judgment. This is the fight in which we are called to engage:

> For our struggle is not against flesh and blood, but against the rulers, against the authorities, against the powers of this dark world and against the spiritual forces of evil in the heavenly realms. Therefore, put on the full armor of God, so that when the day of evil comes, you may be able to stand your ground, and after you have done everything, to stand. Stand firm then, with the belt of truth buckled around your waist, with the breastplate of righteousness in place, and with your feet fitted with the readiness that comes from the gospel of peace. In addition to all this, take up the shield of faith, with which you can extinguish all the flaming arrows of the evil one. Take the helmet of salvation and the sword of the Spirit, which is the word of God. And pray in the Spirit on all occasions with all kinds of prayers and requests. With this in mind, be alert and always keep on praying for all the Lord's people. (Ephesians 6:12 – 18)

Interestingly, the spiritual weapons mentioned in this passage are not autonomous. Each one is beautifully and purposefully dependent on God. Let's consider each one:

- **Belt of Truth**—*dependent* on the fact that the truth of the Gospel of God's grace is the only power that can change a life.

- **Breastplate of Righteousness**—*dependent* entirely on Jesus' righteousness, not our own.

- **Gospel of Peace**—*dependent* on the lifesaving message of the Gospel that promises peace with God.

- **Shield of Faith**—*dependent* on God to meet all our needs.

- **Helmet of a Salvation**—*dependent* on the salvation that God grants through the blood of Jesus Christ.

- **Sword of the Spirit**—*dependent* on God's Spirit to lead and guide us through this dark world as we navigate confusion.

- **Prayer**—*dependent* on seeking God in prayer on behalf of our loved ones.

Fighting the good fight of faith is not being war-like. It does not look like cutting off ears, holding hateful picket signs, calling down fire from heaven, writing scathing posts on social media, or engaging in shaming verbal battles. It is instead leaning (with fear and trembling) into the weapons provided by the Spirit with total dependency on God.

I have personally recognized power in the weapon of prayer and marvel at the fact that, even if someone rejects me, they cannot keep me from praying for them. Nor can they keep the hand of God from moving into their lives because of those prayers. I love this thought! The Bible tells us prayer is powerful and effective. God hears and treasures everyone. The only thing that can interfere with my prayers on behalf of a loved one is my own discouragement.

Although, I would never have chosen the trial of identity confusion, God has mercifully used it to take my faith to deeper levels, away from shallow religiosity.

I close with this sobering thought: There is a real battle raging for our loved ones. What they need most from us is to press into the Gospel on their behalf, not as crusaders out for blood, but as loving ambassadors saved by the Blood. Won't you join me in this good fight? As a mom, I never give up this charge. Since prayer is one of the powerful weapons God invites me to use, I fight through discouragement and pray. In this great season of identity confusion, I anchor my identity firmly in God, who is able to accomplish all that I am not.

> *"Jesus replied, 'What is impossible for people is possible with God.'"*
>
> **LUKE 18:27**

www.ingramcontent.com/pod-product-compliance
Lightning Source LLC
Chambersburg PA
CBHW072205100526
44589CB00015B/2375